The Thunder Dragon Kingdom

THE Thunder Dragon Kingdom

A Mountaineering Expedition to Bhutan

Steven K. Berry

With a Foreword by Chris Bonington

The Crowood Press

Cloudcap • Seattle

Published in Great Britain by
The Crowood Press
Ramsbury, Marlborough
Wiltshire SN8 2HE

British Library Cataloguing in Publication Data

Berry, Steven K.
The Thunder Dragon Kingdom:
a mountaineering expedition to Bhutan.
1. Bhutan. Himalayas. Mountaineering expeditions
I. Title
915.49′8

ISBN 1 85223 146 7

Published in North America by Cloudcap Press
Box 27344, Seattle, Washington 98125

ISBN 0 938567 07 1

Typeset by Avonset, Midsomer Norton, Bath
Printed in Great Britain by Redwood Burn, Trowbridge

Contents

Acknowledgements

The companies and individuals who helped raise the finance for this expedition are too numerous to list here, but especial thanks should be given to those mentioned below as it is from them that the bulk of our assistance came.

Air India
BBC Radio News
BBC TV News
British Mountaineering Council
Terry Daley
John Gau Productions
Jonathan Cape
Mount Everest Foundation

Nova Wholefoods Co-op
Maggie Payne
Reader's Digest
Seton Products
Snow and Rock
Sprayway
The Sunday Times

However, the expedition's greatest thanks must go to those individuals who accompanied us to Base Camp and beyond and who made up our support trekkers. Their friendship and generosity are a special memory.

Dave Carbis
Harry Jensen
Jeremy Knight-Adams
John Knowles

Brian Lee
Tan MacKay
Peter Santamera
Karl Taylor

Patrons

Chris Bonington and Lord John Hunt

Foreword

The hidden kingdom of Bhutan stirs the imagination of all who yearn to travel and explore. Tucked away among the primeval folds of the Eastern Himalaya it takes up little space on a map, even less on a globe, and I dare say that the larger part of our planet's population knows nothing of its existence. Therein lies its appeal. Here is a land to be discovered, mysteries to be unravelled and a culture from which to learn. And, for a very few enterprising and privileged people, there are mountains to be climbed.

It is an unfortunate fact of life that such attractions as those displayed, however unwittingly, by a jewel like Bhutan, may eventually bring about an adverse 'Westernisation' of its people. Such is the case with other Himalayan countries, like Bhutan's larger neighbour Nepal. The flood of tourism has swamped it, each successive wave leaving a higher tide-mark on this slowly disappearing island of untouched beauty. Still they come, on jumbo jets and even Concorde, while King Jigme Singye Wangchuck of Bhutan watches with wise eyes. He has acted on the lesson, and while Bhutan may never realise the fiscal wealth of Nepal, its treasures of culture and landscape remain intact.

Even though tourism is strictly controlled and monitored, Bhutan is treading a fine line. This status quo, built on the ancient beliefs, customs and rituals of the *Drukpa* or Thunder Dragon sect of Buddhism, is like a tall card-house in the middle of a room full of boisterous children. The number of tourists is slowly increasing each year, bringing in vital funds needed for its tentative programme of modernisation. In 1986 Bhutan had some 2,400 tourists. By the end of the century this is predicted to reach 5,000 a year. Demand, however, is much greater, making Bhutan both difficult and expensive to visit. It is little wonder that people should want to go there; who would believe that a land whose gods dwell on mountain tops, where spirits and demons affect the lives of the people, and where reincarnate lamas meditate in musty monasteries amidst mist-shrouded mountains, does actually exist in reality and not just in the pages of some fairy story?

This book is the story of Britain's first mountaineering expedition to Bhutan. Told by its leader, Steven Berry, it encapsulates much of Bhutan's legends, history and way of life, and speaks plainly and honestly about his impressions of the country and its people. This sets it apart from other modern mountaineering literature. Although ultimately unsuccessful, the expedition was a first for British mountaineers. F. Spencer Chapman's ascent of Chomolhari in 1937, hardly qualifies as his two-man party plus Sherpas merely crossed the border from Tibet to start their climb.

The 1986 expedition was certainly well equipped and well prepared for its objective – the south ridge of Gangkar Punsum, the highest mountain in Bhutan and the highest unclimbed mountain available to Western mountaineers. The team's combined experience is impressive, and doubtless would have led them to a successful conclusion had it not been for the great *bête noire* of Himalayan mountaineers, the weather. The strains and tensions of personal relationships are always a focus of expedition stories and this one is no exception. The lack of a tangible reward for all the effort – such as a summit – can only serve to exacerbate tension between climbers. On long expeditions the attainment of the summit is the cleansing fount for spoken and unspoken bitterness towards your companions. Even so, this expedition was, for the most part, a happy one.

Of course, the Bhutanese would not place failure merely at the door of the premature winter winds. For all things, the gods are responsible. They have prevented four expeditions from climbing Gangkar Punsum. The mountains are their dwelling place and they are angry that their sanctity is being invaded, so the Bhutanese have now stopped all expeditions. There is no telling when the mountain gods of Bhutan will again permit an attempt to scale their grandest abode.

It seems indicative of the Bhutanese character that Bhutan's mountain gods should bear no ill will towards their trespassers. The statistics of Himalayan fatalities are the most appalling of all mountain ranges. How is it, then, that not a single mountaineer has died upon Bhutan's highest peak? It is a dark question that does not deserve an answer, but for those who know a little about the Hidden Kingdom, it fits.

Chris Bonington

To Tan MacKay

1
Harry the Camera

When Jeff Jackson and I walked into room 112 in the Motithang Hotel we had been in the Himalayan Kingdom of Bhutan just four days. We were the advance party for the British Bhutan Expedition, whose aim was to make the first ascent of Gangkar Punsum, 24,770ft, the highest mountain in the country. Leaving England on 31 August 1986 we were accompanied initially by our support trek leader, Maggie Mosey Payne, our press officer, Miss Tan MacKay, and Harry Jensen, one of our support trekkers.

Jeff and I parted company from the others in Calcutta as our job was to clear all the expedition equipment through Indian customs. Having accomplished this not inconsiderable task we put the equipment on a truck to be taken overland through the Indian state of Assam and on into Bhutan itself, to Thimphu, the capital. The others had flown on ahead, by the only airline to operate into the kingdom, Bhutan's national airline, Druk Air, which comprised two twin-prop aeroplanes.

The only airstrip in the country is in the steep-sided Paro valley, to the western end of the kingdom, and from there Maggie, Tan, and Harry travelled by car on the only road to Thimphu. Their object in coming out early with Jeff and me had been to complete a warm-up trek before the main expedition group was due to arrive. Their plan had been to trek back over the foothills to Paro, taking four or five days, to coincide with the arrival of the main expedition.

Plans change, and so Jeff and I were not unduly surprised to hear upon our arrival in the capital that Maggie's party were waiting to see us in the Motithang Hotel. As we knocked on the door of room 112 I was keenly anticipating a lot of happy excitement and back-slapping. We deserved to celebrate. Two years of intense struggle and strain had finally brought us to this point – a meeting together in the capital of this mysterious kingdom of the three people who had raised the bulk of the cash for the expedition.

'Come in,' Maggie's Canadian accent drifted through the door.

We walked in and I greeted them with an enthusiastic 'Maggie, Tan, how do you like Bhutan, then? Isn't it incredible?' My voice trailed off. I sensed that something was wrong. Both women sat huddled over an electric fire at the far end of the room. They were covered in mud, their hair was matted, and they were soaked to the skin. Moreover, they looked thoroughly dejected. Tan hardly even looked up; the exuberant response I expected was not forthcoming. Instead Maggie rushed across the room, worry written into the lines of her face. She gave me a hug and said, 'Oh, Steve, something terrible has happened. We've lost Harry.'

It sounded so final, as though he was dead already.

'What do you mean, you've lost Harry? Where is he?' I replied.

Maggie and Tan both started talking at once, contradicting each other in their anxiety and presenting a jumble of incoherent facts.

'OK, OK, just sit down and try and tell me slowly and calmly what has happened, starting from the beginning. One at a time, for God's sake. My brain is likely to blow a fuse at this rate,' I said, trying to inject a note of light-heartedness into the tense atmosphere.

The story poured out. Two days into their warm-up trek they decided to turn back. It had been raining fairly continuously, making the walk a miserable experience, but the decision was mainly because Tan was finding the climb over the high passes very exhausting and was experiencing mild altitude sickness. The crossing from Thimphu to Paro involved two major passes over 11,000ft and the rapid rise to such a height caused her to suffer bad headaches and nausea.

Returning over the Pumo La they started the long descent towards Thimphu, and having passed Pajoding monastery they knew that they were but a few hours from the town. A zigzag track led down through the thick jungle and they mistakenly took an indistinct side path. Tiredness and the promise of a short cut explain the initial mistake but, when the side path petered out, instead of retracing their steps they had decided to carry on downhill through the jungle. Maggie described how they thrashed their way through head-high undergrowth until they heard the sound of a stream. By now they had come so far that they could not face the thought of toiling back uphill again. The stream held the promise of a route through the increasingly dense jungle, and they knew that it must eventually issue into the Thimphu valley. They decided to follow it.

At first it was no more than a burbling brook trickling through the undergrowth, but the further they went the steeper the shallow valley in which it meandered became. Thick bamboos and lush vegetation between the cedars and pines of the forest forced them to clamber along the banks of the stream. After several hours of slow downward progress the valley became so steep and the banks of the stream so precipitous that they were forced to wade through the now rushing water. The valley was rapidly developing into a deep gorge and rock steps appeared in the bed of the stream down which they now slid or clambered.

Maggie made a significant pause in her narrative. She had reached the crux of the story. The two women looked at each other and Maggie waved her hand as much as to say 'You tell him.' Tan leant forward and hesitantly described how frightened they were as the gorge became a more and more serious proposition. Finally they arrived at a boulder the size of a house, which blocked the confined gorge. The stream split either side of it and cascaded down a fifteen-foot drop. Harry negotiated this with considerable difficulty but then there followed an argument. The two women shouted down to him that they refused to go any further, but obstinately he wanted to carry on. They tried their hardest to persuade him of the sense in staying together, Tan said, but he just would not listen. Even when they turned round and started the scramble back up the stream bed he took no notice.

In Harry's defence Tan volunteered the theory that perhaps he was not able to re-climb the drop, or perhaps he could not hear their words clearly above the noise of the stream. Listening to Tan's account, I found myself wondering how I could possibly judge the rights and wrongs of this predicament. I wondered what Harry's side of the story might be. However, whether Harry was right or not in his judgement of the dangers of the gorge made absolutely no difference. He should not have gone further on his own. That much was obvious.

The first time I ever met Harry Jensen was on the outward flight from London to Calcutta, and I formed an impression of a quizzical man with a wry sense of humour. He had a face something like a mandarin, with a drooping moustache and faintly Asiatic features, and usually carried at least three cameras round his neck. We nicknamed him 'Harry the Camera'. An American working as a technician on a body scanner in the main hospital in Riyadh, Saudi Arabia, he was the first person to sign up with our team of eight support trekkers. This disparate group of people were helping to finance the expedition in return for sharing our adventure as far as Base Camp.

Maggie and Tan last saw Harry disappearing down the gorge just after midday. In retracing their steps the two women themselves lost their way again in the jungle. More by luck than judgement, they found themselves, six hours later, at the perimeter fence of the king's palace, to the north of Thimphu.

Now Maggie and Tan sat in steaming clothes, overcome with fatigue and worry, listening to our questions. Where were the search parties going tomorrow? Did they know where the gorge emerged? Were there bears in the forest? How cold was it going to be tonight? Did the Director of Tourism, Jigme Tshultim, know about it? Of course everyone in Thimphu knew by now; in a capital of some fifteen or twenty thousand people news travels fast.

Accompanying Maggie's party had been a Bhutanese guide, Singey Wangchuck, and a small staff of cooks and porters, who had been ten minutes behind the three Westerners. When Singey realised that Maggie had become lost he organised a search party, including members of the king's bodyguard. It was they who found Maggie and Tan, and they had already been out looking for Harry with no success. Darkness had long since fallen and Harry was still missing, with no sleeping bag, dry clothes, or food.

We carried on talking and turning it over until past midnight. Attempting to raise our morale by discussing our first impressions of the Buddhist kingdom failed miserably. We could not lose sight of the real possibility that a man had lost his life. It was the worst possible start to the expedition.

At 2.30 a.m. I jolted awake, clammy with sweat. I had been dreaming. In my dream there was a large party at the hotel to celebrate Harry's return; all the expedition members were there. There was music and laughter. The dream then took a macabre turn. I was called to the back of the building where someone lay under a car trying to change a wheel. The car was jacked up precariously on a slope, threatening to topple over and crush the person underneath. Another person was behind the wheel and suddenly started the engine. The bonnet was raised, and one of my hands was on the idle control. As soon as I let go, the engine revved up and the car tried to move forward, yet the driver would not turn off the engine.

As I woke the significance of the dream dawned on me. I knew what to do about Harry but was not in control of the situation. He was last seen going down a gorge; as he had not appeared, there was a strong chance that he had slipped and fallen over a cliff. Jeff and I, unladen, were climbers, and we had ropes in the Ministry of Tourism stores. In all of Bhutan we were probably the only people qualified to undertake a roped cliff rescue. We would have to descend the gorge ourselves.

I woke Jeff and Maggie. Was I over-reacting? No, they didn't think so; they thought it sounded the best thing to do. The problem was that we would need to leave by first light and would need a Bhutanese guide and the ropes. In the middle of the night Maggie phoned the Director of Tourism to make the arrangements.

By 7.15 a.m. we were joined by Yeshey Wangchuck, the Bhutanese climber appointed to our expedition, and another Bhutanese trekking guide. In the early hours we also collected dry clothing and food for Harry, and all our climbing gear.

The jungle began almost as soon as we left the rear of the hotel, and the path to Pajoding monastery immediately wound unrelentingly up through the forest. It was not long before both rucksacks were being carried by our Bhutanese friends and Jeff and I, unladen, were struggling to keep up with them. Head down, sweat streaming off the end of my nose, I cursed Harry the Camera. A small Tibetan dog followed on our heels as we left the hotel and, try as we might to lose him, he would not leave us.

The forest was mostly tall cedars festooned with hanging lichen and covered in dank mosses. Brightly coloured birds flitted through the thick undergrowth. In just under two hours we reached a stone *chorten* (a religious obelisk), near where Maggie's party had made their original mistake. It was easy to see how they could have been misled, but they should have turned back after thirty or forty yards, where it was obvious that they might be heading for trouble. Once into the gorge, the dog still with us, I could see why they had been reluctant to retrace their steps if it were at all possible to find a way down. With the undergrowth meeting over our heads, we slithered down muddy slopes, clinging

5

to the slippery bamboo. Yeshey, out in front, began yelling and shouting to scare away any lurking bears, and he had brought an ice-axe specifically as defence against them. At this time of year, he told us, brown bears ventured down at night to feast on the apple orchards in the valley, and then retired to the forests to sleep.

We pressed on, and came to the rock where Harry had last been seen. The descent was indeed tricky and the decision to turn back had been correct. Harry was a fool for carrying on. However, the cliffs that I imagined from Maggie and Tan's description of the gorge did not exist. Certainly the going got harder. There were more rock steps, small waterfalls, and the jungle became so thick in places that we were forced to belly-crawl in the stream with an impenetrable wall of bamboo over our heads. The dog was passed hand to hand down the rock steps and waterfalls. I have to admit that we were thoroughly enjoying the adventure as we crashed on down, yelling and laughing. Harry would be OK. He was probably back at the hotel by now having a cool beer, I thought with conviction.

Eventually we heard the roar of a major river ahead. Now we were forced to scramble along the bank above the rapids, sometimes a hundred feet above the noisy torrent. There was only one place where it was conceivable that Harry might have tried to jump from boulder to boulder to the other bank, where the jungle appeared less dense. Jeff and I both thought that such an attempt would have ended in death.

Half a mile further on we came to a slippery-looking log that had fallen across the river. Yeshey was the first across. He straddled the log, the water boiling beneath his feet. When his friend was halfway over, it occurred to me that the only safe way of transporting the dog was in the rucksack on his back. I could not risk calling him over again, and from the far bank they yelled for me to throw the dog across. Picking him up by the scruff of his neck I flung him with all my strength. He fell into the swift water next to the bank and disappeared. Yeshey's friend thrust his hand into the water once, twice – and the second time he held the dog. We all cheered in relief.

On the other side the going became easier, and soon there was a path between banks of flowers. Suddenly a high wire fence appeared and, looking very much out of place, a sentry box. We had arrived at the king's palace. A young sentry leapt out of the box, so surprised at our appearance that he dropped his rifle with fixed bayonet to the ground. No amount of pleading, though, would persuade him to allow us to take the short cut through the grounds. King Jigme Singye Wangchuck was at home. Wearily we set off up the steep hillside, where the perimeter fence plunged back into the forest. Emerging eventually from the trees, we dropped down to some paddy fields, passing a group of houses where we successfully fought off an attack from half a dozen fierce farm dogs. We stopped finally at Wangdi Che monastery on the outskirts of Thimphu and were promptly surrounded by a group of boy monks, who brought us apples. An older, smiling monk approached, offering to take us back to the Motithang hotel in his dilapidated minibus.

The whole rescue venture took us eight hours. Tan was standing on the steps outside the Motithang when we arrived. Her sad expression was enough to tell us that Harry was still missing. He had now been lost for twenty-eight hours. The only conclusion I could draw was that he had been swept away by the river and drowned.

Exhausted, we lay down and slept. An hour later the bedroom door opened and in walked all the other expedition members. They had arrived in Bhutan only a few hours previously and were agog with excitement. The room became packed as other recent arrivals crowded in, including more of the support trekkers. I heard how Jeremy Knight-Adams had missed the plane from London, and of the difficulty the team had had in Calcutta discovering which hotel it was that I had booked them into; this salient fact was omitted from a note that I had left with Bhutanese staff at the airport. I heard with dismay how the bulk of the film gear was still sitting in Calcutta, along with three other expedition bags, as there was not enough room for it on the Bhutanese flight. The good news was that Lydia, not renowned for her organisational ability, had arrived on time from New Zealand. I had not seen her for two years.

'Come on Berry, you lazy dog. Get up. You can't lie around sleeping all day, you know. The film crew want to do an interview with you *now* for BBC news outside the hotel.' Mercilessly Steve Findlay pulled back my bedcovers and threw me my clothes.

Outside the hotel the film crew were setting up their equipment, discussing lighting and angle of shots, and debating whether BBC TV news would be interested in the missing trekker. A small group of Bhutanese hotel staff stood respectfully at a distance and watched us with fascination. I was worried by the thought that Harry's relatives might learn of his disappearance by seeing it on the television or from reading it in a newspaper. I was convinced by now that Harry had been swept away by the river; after all, search parties had been out all day looking for him; even the grounds of the king's palace were searched with the king's express permission. All with no result.

The show had to go on, and the death of this man would fall behind us, but as I tried to act the relaxed, casual role of expedition leader to the camera I felt inwardly extremely disturbed by the thought that a man's death would pass by almost unnoticed. In a few hours I knew that there was a welcoming party arranged by the Ministry of Tourism for the expedition, and there were pressing problems that required immediate attention. I had yet to have a meeting with the Bhutanese authorities to discuss the finances. The rest of the film gear had to be brought on from Calcutta. There were phone calls to be made to sponsors in England, the *Sunday Times* reporter wanted to do an interview, and I had yet to meet some of our other trekkers. What would be their reaction to the news that a companion had been lost and drowned?

At 6.30 p.m. as I was walking down the hotel corridor one of the waiters stopped me and in faltering English said, 'Excuse me Mr Berry la ('la' being the equivalent of 'sir'), your friend is found.'

Could he mean that Harry's corpse had been found, or was he alive after all? The waiter did not know. At the reception desk I discovered that he had been found by a search party, wandering in the jungle, north of the king's palace.

Half an hour later, just as the welcoming party was starting, Harry, looking haggard and tired, arrived to much cheering. The ordeal had been a great shock to his system and he kept himself apart from the rest of us for a couple of days. Maggie and I were both concerned that he had not apologised for the trouble he had caused. I think he was too embarrassed. In any event I needed to obtain from him a note accepting full responsibility in order to clear Singey Wangchuck's name. Although it was clear to me that Singey was not at fault, he faced some criticism from his bosses for losing his charges. The affair had been very much in the public eye, even the king himself was involved, and I was anxious that Singey should not be penalised for a mistake that was not of his making.

Harry was genuinely sorry, but even after his return he had remained largely unaware of the trouble he had caused. The original mistake was probably Maggie's, but had Harry not separated from the women the whole affair would have been merely a minor hiccup, and not the major embarrassment that it had become for both the expedition and the Department of Tourism. However, if nothing else, we learnt a valuable lesson – not to stray off the path in Bhutan.

2
Druk Yul

I possessed a very limited knowledge of Bhutan before a fateful meeting with a Bhutanese colonel in Kathmandu during the spring of 1984. I knew its geographical position – a tiny state sandwiched between Tibet to the north and India to the south, straddling the Greater Himalaya at the eastern end of the chain. I knew that it had been closed to entry from the outside world for centuries and that it was ruled by a young king. I also understood that a few British diplomatic officers had been there in the days of the Empire, and that its people were of Tibetan origin. Very little seemed to be known of its interior, still less about the hundreds of unclimbed, unnamed and unmapped mountains. In short, it seemed a mysterious, unexplored place, with not the remotest possibility of entry.

I had also been told that the only peak that had been climbed was Bhutan's highest – a 24,000ft giant called Chomolhari, conquered in 1937 by an Englishman, F. Spencer Chapman. In those early days I knew only that his ascent had been made from the Tibetan side. I was not to discover until plans were well under way that I had a signed copy of his book, *Memoirs of a Mountaineer*, sitting on my shelves at home unread. It tells a fascinating story of two Englishmen and three Sherpas using hemp rope, canvas tents, tweed jackets and hobnailed boots to climb in a single Alpine-style push one of the highest mountains ever to have been climbed at that time. They were forced to cross into Bhutan to make their ascent and to do this they had the approval of the King of Bhutan as well as of the Tibetan authorities. Only Spencer Chapman and his Sherpa, Pasang, reached the summit, and they were extremely lucky to get down again without losing their lives.

I discovered also that my father had met Spencer Chapman in India after the Second World War and had been given the ice-axe that he had used on Chomolhari. My father had used the axe on his attempt of a mountain called Nun Kun in Kashmir in 1946, and had afterwards donated it to the Himalayan Club in Delhi.

I was well aware of the country's existence, having been born near the border, in Shillong, Assam. I could remember my parents recounting how they had met some Bhutanese government officials in Gangtok, Sikkim, in 1951. Also, in 1981, when unloading boxes into the Air India cargo terminal at Heathrow for my own expedition to Nun Kun, I had noticed that our equipment was stacked next to cases which were addressed to the Queen Mother of Bhutan. I remember thinking at the time that it was a good omen, but my chance to do something positive, to turn idle daydreams into reality, did not come until 1984.

During June 1984, I was resting in Kathmandu after an attempt on the east ridge of Cho Oyu, 26,906ft. Our team had narrowly failed to make the summit, after a gruelling six weeks above the snow line. On the trek out from Base Camp I had thought about Bhutan and idly wondered whether there could possibly be a Bhutanese embassy in Nepal's capital. However, it was accident and not design that led me to meet Colonel Penjor Ongdi on 1 June 1984.

Arriving at Kathmandu, all thoughts of Bhutan disappeared from my mind as I became embroiled in a welter of bureaucratic hassle with the notorious Nepalese Ministry of Tourism. One day a few of us were lounging at our hotel when we received a visit from the Reuters correspondent for Nepal, Liz Hawley. In the past she had provided me with considerable valuable information, and so I casually enquired: 'Liz, you've lived here twenty-five years, what do you know about Bhutan? If ever there was a place I wanted to go, that has to be it. Surely there must be some way of getting in there?'

In chiding tones, like a headmistress admonishing an ignorant pupil, she replied, 'Oh, haven't you met Colonel Ongdi yet? He's Mr Bhutan here in Kathmandu, you know. You do know there's no embassy, I suppose.' I hadn't even discovered that, but didn't feel like admitting it to Liz. She went on: 'If you want to know anything about Bhutan go and see the colonel. He's a nice man. You never know . . .'.

A few days later three of us were walking down Durbar Marg, a wide wealthy street lined with airline offices and good hotels, when, by chance, we spotted Colonel Ongdi's office on the other side of the road. I had almost forgotten the idea of visiting him as there had been more important things to do at the time. The day was so hot, and we felt so lackadaisical, that we almost didn't bother crossing the street. The next two and a half years of my life hinged on that moment.

Having dodged the rickshaws we arrived at a nondescript door with a small brass business plaque. A staircase led to a first-floor office and I noticed with surprise that the handrail was a climbing rope, secured to the wall by pitons driven into the brickwork. The ice-axes, ropes and pictures of mountains that hung on the wall in the reception area confirmed that we were about to meet a man with a special interest in mountains.

The colonel was a well-dressed man in his early sixties, and the strong features of his face differed subtly from those of the Nepalese, hinting at a Far Eastern origin. Even though I was dressed in the most casual of Nepalese clothes he feigned not to notice, and greeted us with the kind of politeness that is the sure sign of a public-school education. We listened with astonishment and growing excitement as he explained that the first three climbing expeditions had been allowed to enter Bhutan the previous year. He himself had been with one of them to their base camp. I was shocked, as there had been nothing about this in the climbing press back home. He went on to say that there were only three peaks available, including a mountain called Gangkar Punsum, 24,770ft. It was still unclimbed. He explained that although many people had believed Chomolhari to be the highest peak in Bhutan this was not the case. Gangkar Punsum was the highest. He gave me a copy of the Mountaineering Rules and Regulations, which he said he had helped formulate, and offered to submit an application on our behalf when next he visited Thimphu.

It was this improbable meeting with a man who seemed influential, at just the right time, that marked the start of the expedition. Had I not met the colonel I doubt that I would have even attempted a task that I already imagined was an unrealistic proposition.

Within two months of my application the precious permit came through, and I became absorbed in reading all the books I could find about Bhutan. Whereas previously I had formed a picture of a mystical kingdom, the more I read the more I found that the history, myths and culture of this forgotten land were in reality even more mysterious than my imagination had led me to think.

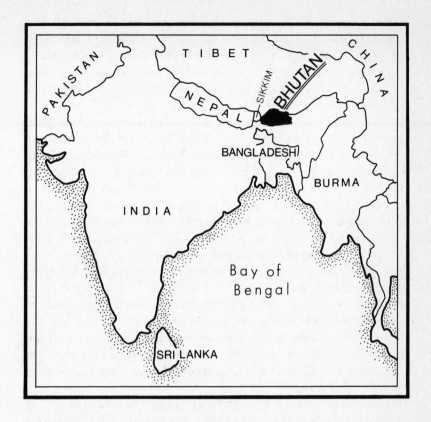

Bhutan – or Druk Yul, meaning 'Kingdom of the Thunder Dragon' – is roughly the size of Switzerland and has an official population of 1.2 million. Its history is roughly traceable to AD 500 or 600, though it is often hard to differentiate between fact and legend. Unfortunately, many of the records, kept in the many monastery/fortresses (dzongs) throughout Bhutan, have been destroyed over the centuries in earthquakes and fires. However it is believed that before the seventh century some of the valleys may have been inhabited by tribes of Indian origin. During a period of a thousand years, roughly from the seventh to the seventeenth century, the Buddhist influence spread from neighbouring Tibet. The first recorded evidence of Buddhism in Bhutan dates from the reign of one of Tibet's most powerful rulers, King Strongtsen Gampo (AD 630–49), when monasteries were built in the valleys of Paro and Bumthang.

Evidence that Bhutan was populated by tribes of Indian origin
is meagre, but the probability is supported by a legend associated
with one of the kingdom's most revered saints, Guru Padma
Sambhava, believed by many Bhutanese to be an incarnation of
Buddha himself. He is also popularly thought to have been the real
founder of Buddhism in Tibet.

The legend has it that early in the ninth century this great
Indian Buddhist sage was invited to visit Bhutan by Sindu Raja, an
Indian who had apparently become King of Bumthang. Sindu
Raja had earlier fled from India and settled in Chakhar,
Bumthang, where he had built himself a nine-storeyed castle of
iron and enjoyed great power. A dispute arose concerning the
border with India and war broke out between Sindu Raja and the
neighbouring Indian ruler, King Nawoche. Although Sindu Raja
is said to have had one hundred wives he apparently had no more
than four children, and one of his sons was killed by King
Nawoche. Sindu Raja was so outraged that he took full reprisal
without first making offering to his guardian spirit. As a result he
offended the gods in the sky, the Naga demons below, and the
spirits of intervening space. They stole away Sindu Raja's soul and
he fell ill. His blood and flesh withered away and only skin and
bones were left. Legend says that his eyes became like stars seen at
the bottom of a well.

No means could be found to cure him, until he was told of
Padma Sambhava, who at that time was lama to King Nawoche.
He was invited to attend Sindu Raja's court, and when he arrived
he meditated for seven days in a cave. The gods became happy and
the spirit guardian gave Padma Sambhava the soul of Sindu Raja
in a pot. The pot was opened in the presence of the Raja and his
soul re-entered his body through his nose, and an intangible
substance having the colours of a rainbow penetrated him through
the top of his head. The Raja was immediately restored to full
health.

Padma Sambhava then interceded between the two kings and
they swore an oath not to cross each other's borders.

A great many legends surround the figure of Padma Sambhava.
Perhaps the most well known is connected with Taksang monastery.
Built high on a vertical cliff face, it marks the spot where he is said
to have landed on the back of a tiger and vanquished five demons
which were stopping the spread of Buddhism.

It is also said that many of Padma Sambhava's teachings, or *termas*, were hidden at times of peril underground or in caves, to be rediscovered in later generations. One of these treasures was discovered at the bottom of a burning lake by a blacksmith living in Bumthang. His name was Pemalingpa and, not knowing how to spread the word contained in the treasures, he hid away, until one night the *Dakinis*, or female heavenly spirits, imparted to him the power to preach. He became a great Buddhist teacher and it is said that when he spoke flowers dropped from the sky and vanished into rays of light. The present dynasty of kings reputedly traces its ancestry to Pemalingpa, who, it is also said, was an incarnation of Padma Sambhava.

The first known Tibetan settlement in Bhutan took place in AD 824, when a Tibetan army was invited into the country to drive out an invading Indian ruler. The latter was driven out and the Tibetan troops decided that they liked the country very much and settled in some of the valleys. A further influx of a large number of Tibetan refugees probably occurred later in the ninth century, when Buddhism suffered severe persecution in Tibet under King Langdarma. The setback to Buddhism in Tibet was only temporary and at the end of that century Indian Buddhist scholars brought about a renaissance in Tibet.

Certainly from that period until the seventeenth century Buddhism continued to spread from Tibet into the Dragon Kingdom. Many sects competed for influence and built monasteries and temples, but it was not until the arrival of the most remarkable man in Bhutan's history, Nawang Namgyal, that the Drukpa sect gained predominance.

Nawang Namgyal was born in 1593 in Tibet. He was descended from a noble family who traced their line to Yeshe Dorje, the founder of the Drukpa sect. While consecrating a new monastery at Ralung, near Lhasa, Yeshe Dorje had heard the sound of thunder in the sky. Popular belief held that this was the sound of dragons, and Yeshe then formed a sect known as the Drukpas. Hence Bhutan's local name, Druk Yul, or Kingdom of the Thunder Dragon.

As a child Nawang had studied at Ralung monastery and claimed to be the incarnation of the famous Drukpa scholar Pema Karpo (1527–92), but the head of the province of Tsang in Tibet had his own candidate for the title, and Nawang was forced to flee

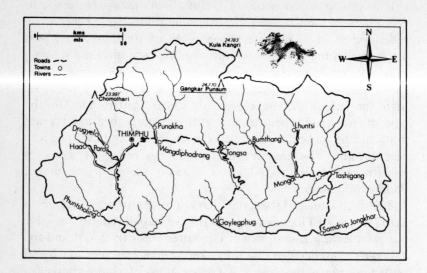

to Bhutan. Legend says that he had a dream in which the protecting deity of Bhutan, Pal Yeshe Gampo, showed him the map of Bhutan and urged him to go there.

Apparently he took with him an image of the Buddha which had been found in the backbone of an important lama in Tibet, and because of this a Tibetan army followed him to Bhutan to effect its recovery. With the help of the local people Nawang repelled the invasion. The head of the Tsang province continued to harass him and it is said that he destroyed him and his family by performing a Tantric ritual.

Nawang Namgyal lived in Bhutan for thirty-five years, dying at the age of fifty-eight. Without doubt he was the most forceful and successful personality of his age, highly gifted and possessing remarkable intelligence. By the end of his life he had united western Bhutan under his rule and four or five years after his death eastern Bhutan was also brought under his system of central government. During his reign, for the first time in several centuries, Bhutan came under attack from the outside. Tibetan armies repeatedly attempted invasion, but under his personal leadership they were all defeated. After his famous victory in 1639 he was afforded the title of Shabdrung Rimpoche, meaning 'at whose feet one submits'. In 1644 and 1647 he also repelled a large army of Mongolians and Tibetans sent by Gushi Khan, the Mogul

16

ruler who had installed the fifth Dalai Lama as sole spiritual and temporal ruler of Tibet. This brought him to the very zenith of his power and he was recognised by all the neighbouring rulers. He even received a gift of a few villages from the King of Ladakh for the purpose of building monasteries there. Ladakh lies at the western end of the Himalayan chain, a distance of some 1,500km from Bhutan. In fact right up until 1958 there was a Bhutanese monk officer stationed in Ladakh to administer their remaining land holdings.

Inside his country the Shabdrung, Nawang Namgyal, consolidated the power of the Drukpas by defeating the other existing Buddhist sects and by building a chain of dzongs to administer the country. Later in his reign he established a dual system of government. He appointed a Jey Khempo, or head abbot, to administer the religious institutions, and a Druk Desi to handle civil matters. The country was divided up into regions, under the governorship of penlops, who exercised their control from the large dzongs. A comprehensive set of laws was written for the first time, based on ten religious and sixteen worldly edicts. He himself composed many famous religious dances, based often on his dream encounters with Bhutan's deities.

It was during Nawang Namgyal's reign that the first Europeans entered the country in 1629. These were two Portuguese Jesuit priests who were *en route* to Tibet. They presented him with some guns and a telescope, which can still be seen at a place called Cheri, just north of Thimphu.

At the age of fifty-eight he retired to a cave to meditate and died shortly afterwards. However, his death was kept a secret by the Jey Khempo for perhaps up to fifty-eight years, for fear that a conflict would break out in the ensuing struggle for power.

A spate of conflicts did indeed break out, as several rivals pressed forward their claim to be the incarnation of the Shabdung. Supreme religious and political power, in theory, rested with the Shabdung, whose successor, or *trulku*, was chosen by incarnation. In practice what happened was that once the Shabdung had been chosen (a process that involved an infant recognising certain possessions of the previous Shabdung) the kingdom was ruled by the Druk Desi until the Shabdung became of age – at which point the Druk Desi was often reluctant to part with his power. The penlops also became virtually independent, having their own armies, and at times were unanswerable to the central authority.

The dual system of government that Nawang Namgyal had set up led to almost continual conflict within Bhutan until the first hereditary monarch was installed in 1907. However, during the century between Nawang's death and the arrival of the British in India, the Bhutanese had become strong enough to make several incursions into both Sikkim to the west and the Indian state of Cooch Behar to the south.

3
The Druk Gyalpos

The first British contact with Bhutan was a violent one. The local claimant to the throne of Cooch Behar sought British assistance and the Bhutanese were driven out by one Captain John Jones with four companies of sepoys and two guns in 1773. Jones also captured three of the Bhutanese frontier forts. The Governor-General of India at the time, Warren Hastings, next received a letter from the Panchen Lama of Tibet, interceding on behalf of the Bhutanese, requesting the end of hostilities. This marked the first discourse between the British and the Tibetans, and Hastings concluded a peace treaty with Bhutan, hoping he could use the opportunity to open trade with Tibet.

Practically all of the next hundred years of Anglo-Bhutanese relations is a story of continual border clashes and of failed trade agreements, culminating in war between the two countries in 1865. In November 1865 the Treaty of Sinchula was signed by both sides. Its aim was to bring about permanent peace and friendship, and in this it succeeded. Under its terms Britain paid an annual subsidy of 50,000 rupees in return for which Bhutan ceded the lands on the Indian plains, agreed to free trade, and allowed Great Britain the right to arbitrate all disputes that might arise.

Bhutan, therefore, retained her independence and the British secured the safety of part of the Empire's frontier. Internal conflict continued within the Dragon Kingdom, but Britain refused to involve itself, concentrating again on its own efforts to secure trade with Tibet. The struggle for power within Bhutan reached its climax at the time of Colonel Younghusband's mission to Lhasa, the capital of Tibet. The power struggle was concentrated between two of Bhutan's district governors, or penlops – the Paro penlop, and a strong man called Ugyen Wangchuck who was the Tongsa penlop. He decided to give every assistance to the British, accompanying them to Lhasa and helping to negotiate the important Anglo-Tibetan accord.

As a result the British made him Knight Commander of the Emperor of India in 1905, and in 1906 he was invited to attend the reception in India for the visiting Prince of Wales. Finally, upon the death of the Druk Desi, a position that still existed but was now weak, Ugyen Wangchuck was invited by the monk body, and all the other chiefs in Bhutan, to accept the title of Druk Gyalpo, meaning Precious Ruler of the Dragon People. On 17 December he therefore became the first King of Bhutan.

The colourful details of Bhutan's history with its tales of reincarnated rulers, mystic forces, of plot and counter plot, and of the British influence in promoting their line of hereditary kings, seduced me from my materialistic Western career. For two years I had worked as a land buyer in the sometimes sordid game of property development, but the work was only a means to an end. I became obsessed with raising the finance for the expedition, and with seeing for myself whether the old mystical kingdom remained under the slow but inevitable advance of the twentieth century. From the time when the monarchy was created change had taken place, and each king had contributed in a series of logical steps to bring Bhutan into the modern world.

The first two kings during their lifetimes sought to unify the country and consolidate the power of the monarchy. Some reforms were started, the second king built a number of schools and dispensaries, but at the time the third king, Jigme Dorje Wangchuck, came to the throne in 1952 the society was still basically feudal. Forced labour, known as *ula*, was common for maintaining the dzongs and for other government work and taxation in kind was a heavy burden on the people. There were no roads, only mule tracks, with the result that each valley had little contact with the others and a journey to the capital from the border with India took six days on horseback. There was no electricity. There was a system of judiciary, though it was often corrupt, and the law was not uniformly applied; the same crime in different parts of the country could have different punishments.

The accession to the throne of King Jigme Dorje Wangchuck was to bring about the largest and most fundamental changes ever seen in the Dragon Kingdom.

It is interesting that since the establishment of the monarchy Bhutan had enjoyed fifty years without any major internal upheavals. All its neighbours had suffered revolutions, military coups, invasion or annexation. In particular Tibet was invaded by China in October 1950, the Dalai Lama forced to flee to India, and the majority of its Buddhist monasteries were destroyed in the name of the Cultural Revolution. Bhutan was greatly affected by this tragic event. Thousands of refugees poured across the border, filling the people with anxiety and disturbing the feeling of security that their isolation had given them for so long.

Need for change became apparent. The new king faced up to the enormous challenge of reforming the whole political system, and slowly opened the doors to modern material progress. He was a truly remarkable man, fifty years ahead of his time. He held dear to his heart the vision of a democratic system of government, in a similar way to his friend and confidant, Nehru, in adjoining India. He was twenty-four when he came to the throne and he died twenty years later having seen much of his dream become reality.

In 1953 he called for a National Assembly to be formed. This comprised 150 members, two-thirds of whom were elected by the people from each of the districts; ten representatives came from the monastic body and certain high government officials were nominated by the king. The Assembly is now the supreme body in the land, enacting laws, approving senior posts in government, and debating freely all issues of national importance.

A Council of Ministers was created, preceded by the establishment of a Royal Advisory Council. Serfdom was abolished. A land-use study and the preparation of ownership records was put in hand. The judiciary was separated from the rest of government and the laws codified. A High Court was brought into being in 1968.

King Jigme Dorje Wangchuck was wholly concerned for the welfare of his people; he wished to secure their safety from ambitious China, to bring them freedom and justice, and to introduce the good things from the modern world outside. At the same time he held above all things the importance of maintaining intact the ancient traditions and cultural values. Bhutan remained virtually closed to the outside world, and only a handful of foreign visitors were granted entry during his reign. He was a man loved by his people and, although still held in awe – believed by many to be literally a living god – he broke down some of the old archaic customs. For instance, those entering his presence no longer had to prostrate themselves before him. He was so concerned with the principle of democracy that in 1969 he relinquished his right to veto the National Assembly's decisions. By so doing he had voluntarily given up his position as absolute monarch.

The king did not interfere with the religious order; the Jey Khempo continued to hold full authority concerning religious matters and his status to this day is second only to that of the king. Much of the cost of the dzongs and lamas falls on the government, though it is supplemented from property owned by the monasteries and from gifts from the people.

Ties with India were strengthened, particularly with the commencement of a road from the border to Thimphu in January 1960. In fact at the time of the initial negotiations in India regarding building the road special prayers were offered in all the monasteries in Bhutan for their successful conclusion. The following year saw the first of Bhutan's five-year development plans. Schools and hospitals were built, a national postal system, connected to the outside world, was created. Telephones were installed, paper money was introduced, and in addition to the road from India work was started on several hydroelectric projects. This included the massive Chukha dam, now exporting electricity to India. India supplied, initially, all the engineers and technicians to make these things possible, providing 600 million rupees for the first ten years.

The Sinchula Treaty of 1865 had already been replaced, after Indian independence, by a fresh Indo-Bhutanese treaty in 1949. This gave back to the Bhutanese an area of land taken by the British, called Dewangiri, increased the annual subsidy to half a million rupees, and again provided for free trade. In signing the treaty, India accepted Bhutan's status as a completely independent state.

In a typically far-sighted move Jigme Dorje had opened the eyes of the rest of the world to the very existence of Bhutan by joining the United Nations in 1971, and had started a process of seeking limited financial aid from other world bodies and other nations.

In just twenty years Jigme Dorje, third Druk Gyalpo, had transformed the medieval, feudal state into a stable nation with a democratic system of government, where the interests of the people were paramount. With skill and patience he convinced his subjects of the wisdom of ending their centuries of splendid isolation.

This had been no easy task, and clashes between dissenting parties had resulted in the assassination of his Prime Minister in 1964. However, he won his arguments and went on to form a special relationship with India to augment the changes.

On the evening of 21 July 1972 he died in Nairobi at the age of forty-four. The grief inside their small, close-knit country was devastating. He had been like a father to them all, they had become so used to him driving around in his open-top jeep smiling and talking to any of those he met. His body was flown home and held, embalmed, in the capital for eighty-nine days, allowing his countrymen time to pay final homage. Every day his meals were served as usual, and prayers were offered at his bier without ceasing until the day of his cremation. Only his close family and Indira Gandhi, a special guest, actually attended the final ceremony, which took place in Bumthang. However, more than ten thousand people in the valley lined the route for several miles, showering flower petals in his path.

His son, King Jigme Singye Wangchuck, whose name translated means Fearless Lightning Lion, has carried on his father's work, and like him is said to be a man mature beyond his years. His Foreign Secretary once said: 'I have known His Majesty from the time he was in diapers, yet when I go before him now I feel as though I stand before my grandfather.' At the age of thirty-two he is the youngest of the twenty-nine ruling monarchs left in the world today.

He was educated at Darjeeling in India, and for two years at Heatherdown Preparatory School in England. As a young man he worried his elders by going rock climbing in the local hills and by racing his Japanese motorcycle around Bhutan's mountain roads. Such is the sense of equality in Bhutan that he used to play billiards in the local community centre. Today his sports are a little more restricted. He plays basketball with members of his bodyguard; if he makes a bad shot everyone looks the other way. He also plays golf with his first cousin, Dasho Penjor Dorji, a man who is known throughout Bhutan as 'Bengy'. Occasionally he goes hunting for tiger in the forests to the south, the only person allowed to do so, and he is apparently adept at the national sport of archery.

He is unmarried, which causes great concern to his people as it is imperative that he has an heir. When questioned on the subject by an Asian newspaper in September 1985 he replied: 'Yes, I'm under heavy pressure to choose a queen. I guess I'll have to do something about that very soon.'

He lives a reasonably austere life. His palace is a small log house in secluded grounds just outside the capital, where he lives with a personal bodyguard of about forty men. He did have a Rolls-Royce but rumour has it that it was always going wrong so he gave it to the Foreign Ministry. He can now be seen driving around the capital in his green Range Rover. His personal mechanic is a Ghanaian, one of only two Africans in the country at the time we were there. The king's one indulgence is smoking fat Havana cigars, sent to him by Fidel Castro himself. He rarely goes abroad and said once, 'I think the best place to have a holiday is Bhutan itself.' He never wears Western clothes, preferring the traditional *kho* – even when he plays basketball he just folds the sleeves back so that he can throw properly.

He sometimes travels to many of the remote parts of his kingdom, talking to the people, explaining his policies and listening to their views. Any citizen may approach him and present a petition, called a *kidu*, which is always assured of a royal response. Like his father he firmly believes that 'progress can only be truly achieved with the support and participation of all the people'. His highest priority is making the kingdom self-reliant and maintaining its cultural heritage.

He is well known for having stated that the people's gross happiness is far more important than the gross national product. In 1984 the annual *per capita* domestic income was thought to be only $160 per person, making Bhutan one of the poorest nations in the world, but this is an entirely unrealistic picture: first, because in many parts of the country barter is still the method of exchange, and, second, no one really knows accurately what the population is.

In the fourth month of the Wood-Tiger year, at the auspicious hour of the Serpent – 2 June 1974, at 9.10 a.m. – Jigme Singye Wangchuck's coronation took place in the Tashichhodzong (seat of government). He picked up his great grandfather's five-coloured scarf which only he and the Jey Khempo are ever allowed to touch, and putting it round his shoulders became the fourth Druk Gyalpo. For the first time foreign press were allowed in to record the event, and of the handful of foreign dignitaries even China, the oppressor of Tibet, had a representative. The British High Commissioner in Delhi, Sir Michael Walker, committed a rather embarrassing *faux pas* at the celebrations afterwards when, given an opportunity to try his hand at archery, he shot a bystander through the leg. The king dismissed the incident with a regal 'Don't worry, these things happen all the time.'

The young king quickly earned the respect of his government officials, who never know at what time of the night he might call them for facts and figures or other information. No one ever remembers him losing his temper, but he has a reputation for having a sharp, incisive mind and a remarkable memory. The highest officers we met held him in the greatest esteem, and no one attends an audience with him without being well prepared.

Viewed from the outside world Bhutan is proceeding with her development slowly and carefully, avoiding the problems caused in Nepal. When Nepal opened its doors to mass tourism it suffered as a result a drugs problem, corruption within government, and a wholesale dilution of its culture. Nevertheless, the changes as seen from within Bhutan are dramatic. There is now a narrow airstrip at Paro receiving almost daily flights from Calcutta; there is a bus service connecting the main valleys, a national radio, broadcasting every day, and a national weekly newspaper. There is a banking service and a handful of new hotels, and trade with India, along the relatively new road, has brought about a large building programme of shops and houses. In the five-year plan to 1991, 500 million rupees are to be spent. Of this, 40 per cent is provided by India, 30 per cent is raised from internal sources, and the balance comes from Australia, Switzerland, Japan, Great Britain, Singapore, New Zealand, Austria and various world bodies.

The striking thing in Thimphu is the large numbers of foreign aid workers. There are research and development projects under way throughout the country associated with animal husbandry, crop studies, irrigation, forestry, mineral surveys, education, small-scale industrial development – the list is almost endless. Consultants and advisors throng the government offices pressing for this plan or the other; the hotels become venues for all manner of government planning meetings.

In 1974 the king allowed the first trickle of tourists to enter the kingdom and by 1986 foreign visitors had still reached only 2,405 annually. The number is slowly rising but is strictly controlled, and being a tourist is expensive. Even with such small numbers tourism is the single highest earner of foreign capital for Bhutan. Foreign earnings are needed to redress the imbalance in their trade figures and to service their loans, and projects are springing up to increase their exports in an effort to minimise the reliance on tourism.

For all these changes, life for the majority of the people is little affected. Bhutan after all is a Himalayan kingdom whose people live a rural life in small villages in remote valleys. Their Buddhist culture and their isolation from a turbulent world seem to have preserved a natural, innocent happiness that King Jigme Singye Wangchuck has every right to protect.

4
Thimphu

On 31 August 1986 Jeff Jackson and I, accompanied by Maggie, Tan and Harry the Camera, boarded the Air India flight via Rome, Bombay and Delhi for Calcutta. The two intervening years since meeting Colonel Ongdi had been a traumatic time. The climbing permit had been cancelled and was only reissued six months before our departure. The reason for this had been that when an American climbing team had failed even to find Gangkar Punsum, in the autumn of 1985, they had demanded their money back from the Bhutanese authorities, claiming that they had been misled regarding the route to the mountain. They had also promised to give Bhutan bad press at a 'Bhutan night' sponsored by the American Alpine Club to be held in New York on 7 December 1985. Upon hearing this the king had called an inquiry, during which all climbing permits were cancelled, including ours. Intensive lobbying on our part and a change of attitude by the Americans, we think, caused our permit to be reissued, though the internal workings of the government in Bhutan were for us, then, as great a mystery as the kingdom itself.

Also at about the time that the permit was reissued a conflict of personalities erupted between myself and Doug Scott. Early in 1985 Doug had asked if we would include him in the team. We had felt honoured to have with us this Everest summiteer and world-renowned Himalayan climber, affectionately regarded as the John Lennon of the climbing world, with his pebble glasses and long hair. However, he and I spent the whole time arguing about what was to be done and how to do it, and after considerable soul searching Doug decided to withdraw from the expedition. This was a great loss from a climbing point of view, and if I am honest it was a major loss to our ability to attract publicity. However, from my own personal point of view the greatest trauma was in the conflict itself and not its consequences. Doug's decision had not been made lightly; he had put considerable effort into helping unlock our permit, and badly wanted to visit Bhutan to further his knowledge of Buddhism.

However, money was the main worry and 80 per cent of the £40,000 needed to fund the expedition entered the account in the last three months before departure, the balance being mainly expedition members' personal contributions. The last major cheque, a sum of £6,400 arrived with only five days to go. All Himalayan expeditions seem to scrape the money together at the last minute, though consoling oneself with this unwritten law does not alleviate the strain when the money is not actually in the account.

Jeff and I stayed four days in Calcutta clearing customs. We were given a room in Bhutan House, a semi-derelict palace on the outskirts of the city that had belonged to the late Prime Minister of Bhutan. Its large, empty, marble-floored rooms and its marble swimming pool, now full of dirty water had, before the assassination of the Prime Minister in 1964, been a staging post for him and the royal family in their diplomatic journeys outside Bhutan. It is used now as a store and residence for a small number of Bhutanese customs officers. We were grateful to our new Bhutanese friends for providing us with a haven from the chaos and squalor of India's most crowded city.

On 5 September we boarded Druk Air's 7.50 a.m. flight to Paro, Bhutan. Taking off from Dum-Dum airport, the seventeen-seater twin-prop Dornier rose steadily above the fertile patchwork of fields irrigated by one of the world's largest rivers, the Brahmaputra. We could see its thick silver shape, fed by innumerable tributaries, twisting its lazy way towards the Bay of Bengal. The late monsoon clouds hid the Himalayan range to the north, though the pilot, turning in his seat, told his passengers that the faint smudge of white on the horizon was Everest, the only peak high enough to break the clouds. The plane droned on over the Indian plains for two and a half hours at a height of 11,000ft. From an urn on the floor in the rear of the plane Jeff served coffee to the other passengers, a mixture of Indian businessmen, foreign aid workers, and Bhutanese government officials.

Eventually an unbroken line of dark hills rose sharply in front of us and a few minutes later we were entering a deep valley. The plane became an insignificant wasp towered over by wooded mountainsides clad in puffy clouds. We had reached the Bhutanese foothills. Waterfalls cascaded down cliffs and a ruined dzong passed by below. I wondered whether it was one of the frontier forts that Captain Jones had captured in 1773. The aircraft turned left at a junction of two rivers into a steeper sided valley, forced to bank quite sharply round rocky bends. Suddenly the valley broadened. Immediately ahead was a narrow tarmac runway, and beyond that I could see through the cockpit window the massive square bulk of Paro Dzong. The ancient fortress completely dominated a flat and highly cultivated valley floor, dotted with houses which looked like Swiss chalets. The roar of the aircraft engines increased, and I registered that people in the fields were waving. There was a final crescendo of noise, a few seconds of anxiety that all was not as it should be, and then we had touched down and were throttling back. All the passengers clapped loudly.

In the small airport building sunshine poured through the windows and half a dozen dragonflies hovered and flitted amongst us as we waited for our visas to be stamped in our passports. The building's walls, ceilings, and intricately carved wooden eaves were all painted with tantric symbols. We had been transported from the sticky, humid heat and the frenetic rush of life in India to a different world. Here the Bhutanese officials greeted us with relaxed smiles, their deep-set Mongolian features creasing with merriment at the sight of Jeff's 'helicopter' hat and his extrovert behaviour. Their unique national dress, a cross between a kilt and a robe with long sleeves and wide white cuffs, often made from material closely resembling tartan weave, gave them a regal appearance. Here there was none of the indifference or ineptitude of the Indian official.

Outside in the sunshine Kangdu Dorji, one of Bhutan's handful of climbers, trained in Japan, welcomed us in well-spoken English. Almost the first piece of information he imparted was the fact that the Japanese team would not be coming this year to attempt Gangkar Punsum. This was excellent news. We had expected them to be on the mountain at the same time as ourselves. It meant that we would probably be given the south ridge, which we had wanted all along. However, I was greatly surprised when he told me that an Austrian team had just failed on the south ridge. I had understood that their expedition had been postponed. They had obviously tried to steal a march on us. I felt it was a desperate measure indeed to have gone there in the monsoon.

Kangdu Dorji took us by car to the Olathang Hotel, built two years earlier high on a hillside overlooking the Paro valley. As we drove the two miles from the airstrip we passed an old man wearing a cane hat, rather Chinese in style, and spinning a hand-held prayer wheel. His short bows to our passing car conveyed an attitude of respect. We passed a group of women and children, dressed in brightly coloured clothes and carrying large bundles of straw on their backs. They all stopped and waved, smiling and laughing happily. Upon reaching the hotel we were surprised to find the manager and a number of his staff on the steps waiting to greet us. I have never encountered such friendliness in a country before.

In the construction of the Olathang's main building, completed two years ago, no slackening of traditional methods or design had been allowed. It was built in a square around a central garden, and like the dzong its massively thick stone walls were painted white and tapered slightly. The heavy timbered eaves were colourfully painted with the same Buddhist symbols we had seen at the airport and on the houses along the way. On the wall panels inside were hand-painted pictures, a recurring theme being the royal crest, a circular design of two coiled dragons, crossed *vajras* (diamond sceptres) and gemstones. Heavy wooden beams and richly carved chequered cornices were all picked out in appropriate religious patterns. A framed picture of all four of Bhutan's kings hung above the reception desk.

A number of thatched wooden chalets blended into the groups of pine trees surrounding the hotel. Cows with bells round their necks grazed on the lawns in between. To our great pleasure Jeff and I discovered we had been reserved a chalet each. Inside, Tibetan rugs lay on the floor, and the windows were hung with bright blue, red and yellow silk curtains, like hangings in a monastery. The European-style furniture was draped with fine Bhutanese cloth. We were used to a rather poorer standard of accommodation on our expeditions and the first-class treatment came as something of a shock.

In the afternoon our guide took us to visit Paro Dzong. At the beginning of the tenth century a much smaller monastery had stood where now stands the fortress built by Nawang Namgyal in 1646. Its outer walls taper like that of the Potala in Lhasa, Tibet, and are six storeys high, whilst its central tower rises at least a further four storeys above the red roof of the outer wall. Its ancient, enormous bulk put me in awe, and I found myself speaking in subdued tones as we wandered round its courtyards and galleries. I strongly felt a sense of timelessness; only the most drastic event would ever change anything here – an earthquake, a war, or a major fire. Young monks dressed in deep-red robes gathered round us, keen to look through the zoom lens of my camera. Others sat cross-legged, swaying and chanting mantras and reading from rectangular loose-leaved prayer books. A few lay on windowsills asleep in the sun. A gong sounded and an elder monk appeared carrying a leather whip. Fingering a rosary of ivory beads, he thrashed the whip on the wooden floor, at a spot worn away by centuries of ritual. The boy monks drifted over and then trooped off to some closed ceremony. Once a year, at the five-day spring *tsechu* (religious festival), one of the most important events in Bhutan's religious calendar takes place at Paro – the unfurling for a few hours before daybreak of the sixty-foot square scroll painting called Thongdel. It is believed that those who set eyes on it receive great merit in their quest for nirvana and the resulting escape from the wheel of life.

Outside again we walked down a stone-flagged path to the cantilevered bridge next to the dzong. On the way an old man posed for us, his mouth stained red from chewing betel nut, and then held out his hand for money. We feigned ignorance of his motive, pretending we thought he was making a joke. I was conscious that here possibly was the first sign of Western influence. The old man withdrew his hand in embarrassment, but stayed with us, and we continued to enjoy each other's company, though I wondered sadly how long it might be before Westerners would be viewed principally as a source of income rather than as people. How long would it be before a refusal to pay would be greeted with a show of unfriendliness, such as is the case in Nepal and India? It was, in actual fact, the only time we experienced even this half-hearted form of supplication.

Jeff complained of feeling slightly ill and we returned to the hotel. At 7 p.m. I sauntered over to his chalet and found him almost delirious. He was shaking so badly his teeth chattered uncontrollably and he was pouring sweat. He was able to manage a sentence or two of coherent speech before lapsing into delirium.

I grasped that the fever had hit him without warning and that he felt as though there was electricity coming out of his hands, feet and head. He asked me where the men had gone, and when I asked him which men he meant he told me that there had been some men in the room who had erected a palm over him, to shade him from the sun, and that they had put leaves in his mouth. I told him he was imagining things, and sent for the doctor.

When the doctor arrived he told me that it was a common enough complaint in the valley, and reassured me that it would not last long – a day or two, probably. He advised me not to mention the men and the palm tree to the hotel boys as there was strong belief in spirits in the valley and it would only fuel gossip. I slept on the settee that night and the manager of the Olathang insisted that one of his boys sleep on the floor, in case he was needed. Jeff continued to spout delirious babble most of the night.

Within two days, remarkably, he had made a full recovery and felt fit enough to accompany me to Taksang monastery, seven miles to the north-west. Clinging to its granite cliff thousands of feet above the valley floor, it is reached by a narrow path along a series of ledges on the cliff face. The marks where Padma Sambhava landed on the back of a tiger are imprinted in the rock inside the monastery. A more mystical place for such a mystical event would be hard to imagine. Semitropical jungle lay far below in the valley and spilled over the tops of the cliffs above, prayer flags fluttered, and misty clouds swirled around the temple. Monks chanted, temple bells tinkled.

That evening, back in Paro, I walked up the hill behind the hotel to enjoy the spectacular scenery. To the north, behind the high ridges of the wooded foothills, there were glimpses of snow-capped peaks. The valley below, perhaps two miles wide, was a patchwork of rice paddies, wheat fields and scattered settlements. The Paro Chu river, running down from the glaciers near Chomolhari, flowed quietly past the brilliant white edifice of the dzong. Three inquisitive eagles circled above my head, literally only thirty feet above me. These relaxing days in Paro, adjusting to the shock of a different culture, had been an ideal start to our adventure, but now I felt keen to move to the capital and begin the round of important meetings with the Ministry of Tourism.

On 8 September we drove to Thimphu. Leaving the floor of the lush valley behind, the road traversed a steep rocky hillside in a series of never-ending hairpins. After half an hour we reached the confluence of the Wang Chu and Paro Chu rivers. White and red chortens stood on the opposite bank; more prayer flags on tall poles set their magic messages adrift on the wind. A team of Indian roadworkers laboured in the dust repairing a road after a minor landslide. The road now started a long climb, twisting and turning above the Wang Chu. Our driver was a cautious man; there are only 2,500 registered vehicles in the Dragon Kingdom but the bends were blind, the road narrow, and the drop to the river daunting. Occasionally we passed groups of houses, red chillies drying on the wood shingle roofs, straw packed in under the eaves, their dark woodwork gaily painted with the symbols of their religion. Wherever land could be terraced, irrigated and cultivated, tiny communities had sprung up.

Guarding the entrance to the Thimphu valley stands the oldest fort in Bhutan, Simtokha Dzong. It stands astride a projecting ridge with a commanding view over the approaches to the valley. Five miles away and slightly below us we could make out the main township, spread widely either side of the river. The valley was similar to Paro, enclosed by 12,000 or 13,000ft Himalayan foothills running in ridges north to south, strangled in thick jungle for the most part. The toes of subsidiary ridges crept out on to the flat, highly cultivated, valley floor. The tops of the ridges were covered in cloud and the occasional shower wetted our windscreen.

As we approached the capital a helicopter flew overhead, bringing the king home from his attendance of the summit in Harare, Zimbabwe, of the Pact of Non-Aligned Countries. Apparently, whenever the king flies in all his most important advisors meet him at the helipad to welcome him home.

We gave a ride into town to a couple of monks, whose betel-stained mouths matched the colour of their robes. I was rather bemused, as they had been walking away from Thimphu, but on sight of us at the side of the road obeying the call of nature they had hopped into the car, seemingly content to travel in the reverse direction to that which they had intended.

The one object that was predominant, seen glinting in the sun at some distance from the town, was a three-storeyed chorten, capped with a circular, pointed, gold top-piece. It had been built to the memory of the late king, Jigme Dorje Wangchuck (reigned 1952–72). We crossed the river by a modern Bailey bridge bedecked in white, yellow, and green prayer flags, and passed through a checkpost manned by soldiers in blue serge uniforms. Our car did not even slow down.

There was still practically no traffic, and townspeople either looked at us inquisitively or responded to our perhaps infectious excitement by waving. I was expecting a crowded, busy city, as most capitals are in the East; instead I found we were driving down wide streets with sycamores or willow trees shading the pavements, where people strolled rather than jostled. Thimphu is the main shopping centre in the kingdom, but there is none of the ramshackle atmosphere of a bazaar; the shops are pristinely clean and highly carved and decorated, in neatly ordered rows. I was encouraged on seeing how little Westernisation had taken place. The vast majority of the populace wore national costume. Almost universally they now wear Western-style shoes, which have replaced the felt and leather boots with upturned toes, now worn only on ceremonial occasions. The women returned our smiles, unconcerned at our taking their photographs. Their black hair was cropped short and they wore no nose jewellery. The ankle-length dresses and highly embroidered silk jackets were made of the finest-weave material in richly colourful patterns. Round their necks they wore heavy necklaces of turquoise, coral and silver. Their beautiful Tibetan-like features were marred somewhat by the habit of chewing betel.

Their confident behaviour is the result of a strongly egalitarian society where women can enjoy a high degree of equality. They have the right to vote, they can initiate divorce, choose whom they like to marry, and often hold high office in government. The sons do not necessarily inherit the family estates; land and property is often divided between sons and daughters.

There are plenty of modern goods for sale – radios, tape recorders and other electrical items, even the digital wrist watch and calculator have found their way into Bhutan. The most disturbing thing, I thought, was the presence of a small video shop. The bulk of the films in the window were trashy Western violence. With no television in the country, TV sets and videos have to be specially imported at great cost. I also later met two young educated Bhutanese who knew more about what was top of the pops in America, and more about the private lives of film stars, than the rest of our party put together.

The character of the town is not adversely affected as yet by tourism. There were only two souvenir shops, plus a government emporium. The two cinemas showed mainly Hindi movies, and there were no restaurants for eating out. The four decent hotels in town all had good food, however, and whilst we were there we discovered that there was a constant round of parties and dinner evenings amongst the many development aid workers who lived in Thimphu.

Thimphu stands at an altitude of 7,600ft and has been the permanent capital since 1955. During the winter it can become very cold and is snowed up three or four times a year. Many of the wealthier families move to the lower valley of Paro when the cold weather arrives. The town has expanded during the last twenty years, as the nation's modernisation plans have brought a need for more government offices and housing. In addition, the road from the Indian border, started in 1960, has produced many new shops as trade with India has developed. The results of this expansion could have been disastrous but the king, anxious to preserve the culture of his kingdom, has insisted that all new buildings are built to traditional design.

We passed through the clean streets of the capital, swept twice a week, and just as we were passing an open field where some boys were practising the national sport, archery, the driver stamped on the brakes and the car slewed to a halt, forty-five degrees to the curb.

'What's happening?' I said, thinking we had run over a dog.

'We must stop for the princess, Berry la,' was the reply. One of the royal family passed by in the opposite direction in a BMW.

All Bhutanese defer to authority with marked respect, not in any obsequious way but as part of an old-world etiquette. An illustration of this high degree of politeness was the way the traffic police behaved. There were two of them, one either end of the town, dressed in white uniform and matching topee. With so little traffic there was never any danger of collision, but the two men took their duties extremely seriously. As each car approached it was waved on with the most elaborate hand signals, and a silver whistle was blown continuously. Their performance was more like a dance than anything connected with traffic. One day we had to wait behind another car at one of these junctions and the policeman apologised with a sorry expression and shrug of the shoulders.

The Mountaineering and Trekking Department had locked all our equipment into their store; it had arrived that day on a truck from India. I was relieved, not to say astonished, that it had passed through India without a hitch. Before moving up to the Motithang Hotel (where we were to discover that Harry the Camera was missing) Jeff and I were introduced to Yeshey Wangchuck, Bhutan's most experienced climber, who was to join us as climbing partner and liaison officer. He was a tall, handsome man and employed as Assistant Manager at the Mountaineering and Trekking Department. We struck an immediate rapport, particularly once we had rescued and opened one of our bottles of Glenfiddich whisky from the expedition equipment. It was whilst the three of us were engaged in making toasts to our success on the 'White Peak of the Three Spiritual Brothers' that a call came through that Maggie and Tan had returned from their aborted trek to Paro.

5
Dremos and Tsechus

On the morning following Harry's reappearance from the jungle I was due to give an interview for Bhutan national radio. Yeshey and a driver arrived promptly at the hotel and drove Tan and me through pouring rain to a small building near the main fortress, the Tashichhodzong.

Tan MacKay was the expedition's voluntary press officer. Middle-aged, with a stern, almost imperious appearance, she had a commanding presence which hid, only briefly, a kind and generous nature. Normally she worked as chief press officer for *Reader's Digest* and had become involved when one of my begging letters had accidentally landed on her desk. The previous year she had spent a month in Tibet, and at the prospect of visiting Bhutan she had unstintingly thrown herself into the task of gaining us publicity. She had become so involved that she had literally given herself ulcers at the time when the expedition was at the brink of folding for lack of cash.

The detached two-storeyed radio building – with its own garden, covered porch and lack of public notice-boards – was more like a private house than a transmitting station. We were met by Louise Dorji, an Englishwoman who is one of a handful of permanent foreign residents. She wore Bhutanese national dress and her black hair was cut short like that of the local women. I thought her touching politeness was a Bhutanese mannerism she had unconsciously adopted. As we talked I discovered that we were only the twelfth climbing expedition to visit the kingdom, and were the subject of much talk in the town, not only because of the Harry the Camera episode but also, since we numbered twenty-two Europeans, because we were far larger than any other expedition to have visited Bhutan.

We were ushered upstairs to a room containing only a table and a few chairs. The recording equipment was a pocket-sized Sony tape recorder and a hand-held mike. The sound of traffic drifted through the open window, and occasionally, as the interview proceeded, people tiptoed in and out of the room, their conspiratorial smiles showing that they too were quite amused by the primitive equipment. On adjacent land a new 50kW transmitter and offices for daily broadcasts were being built but sitting there that morning in a room decorated with Buddhist symbols, drinking salted tea, I felt keenly the sense of being in a forgotten corner of the world.

The interview was pleasant and informal. Yeshey and I took it in turns to answer the questions that fascinate people the world over, about why climbers want to risk their lives on Himalayan mountains. Listening to Yeshey's replies I learnt that he was the only climber in Bhutan who had been on Gangkar Punsum. He had been there with the Japanese the previous year and had reached Camp 2 with them. His knowledge of the route, its difficulties, and places for camps would be invaluable to us, saving us time we could not afford to waste.

Afterwards I was chauffeured downtown to the offices of the Bhutan Tourism Corporation (BTC), which were housed above some shops off the main square. I was to meet Jigme Tshultim, Director of BTC, and to pay over the money we owed for the cost of the expedition, approximately £30,000 for seven climbers for a period of sixty days within the country. Bhutan has devised a system for mountaineering expeditions that has copied the best principles from the procedures in operation in Nepal, China, India and Pakistan; the visiting team pays a fixed dollar rate per person for each day the expedition is in the country. This charge includes everything bar food above Base Camp. It covers porterage to and from Base Camp, all road transport, hotel accommodation, a trekking staff including a radio operator, and a mail runner. There are no customs fees or desperate bureaucracy to deal with, as there are in Nepal. If there was a problem we talked it over with either Jigme or, more likely, Karchung Wangchuck, Manager of the Mountaineering and Trekking Section.

Jigme Tshultim was an important man, in control of all aspects of tourism, the only person with higher authority being the Deputy Minister for Tourism and Communications, Dasho K. Letho, who like all ministers had his offices in the Tashichhodzong. I was looking forward to meeting Jigme as we had been corresponding, on and off, for two years. He was a jovial man with an impish sense

Above *Gangkar Punsum from Base Camp just after sunrise. (Photo: Steven Berry)*

Below *Misty mountains in the foothills. (Photo: Steven Berry)*

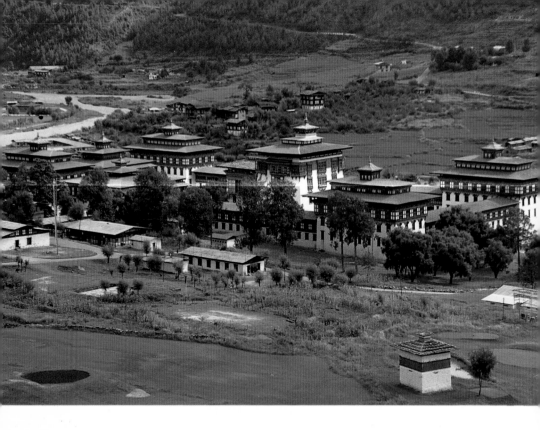

Above *The Tashichhodzong, Thimphu.*
(Photo: John Knowles)

Left *Bhutanese children – note the*
prayers painted on the wall behind them.
(Photo: Harry McAulay)

of humour, but his deportment was that of a man in a powerful position. In a happy, relaxed atmosphere we talked for an hour and a half, amongst other things about why the Japanese had pulled out at the last minute. There had been some trouble with an outstanding payment for the helicopter rescue of one of their climbers who contracted hepatitis at Base Camp in 1985. The money had been paid recently, but its late arrival had meant that the Japanese had postponed their expedition. The American team, approaching the mountain from a different direction the same year, had never actually reached Gangkar Punsum, and Jigme recounted amusingly how they had spent much of their time trout fishing instead.

However, we were not without our own problems. The bulk of the film gear and Jeremy Knight-Adams were still stuck in Calcutta. Because of the clouds covering the foothills for the last few days, Druk Air had not been able to get through. This is a fairly common occurrence and passengers are known to spend days waiting in Calcutta for a flight, during which time a build-up of passengers just makes the situation worse. Karchung was making strenuous efforts to get the gear on an Indian Airlines flight to Bagdogra, near the border, from where it would be picked up by a Bhutanese truck and brought to the capital. What would happen to Jeremy we really weren't quite sure. Assam being a restricted area within India, he could not accompany the truck.

Ours was a complicated expedition split basically into three groups: the climbers, the trekkers, and the film crew, plus a *Sunday Times* reporter. There was a danger here that, because each group had its own particular interests, conflict was possible. We now encountered a situation which exposed the potential for difficulties between us. Our original plan had been to spend one day in the capital before leaving by road for Bumthang, where we would transfer our loads to horses for the start of the walk-in. Now we were forced to wait, for how long we did not know, until the film gear caught up with us. Coincidentally in three or four days' time the *tsechu*, the main yearly religious festival, was due to take place in the Tashichhodzong, and the film crew wanted to delay our departure in order to film it.

The majority of the climbers wanted to get moving towards the mountain. We knew we only had sixty days within Bhutan and four days was an important loss. The trekkers, without exception, said that whatever the climbing team wanted to do they were happy to fall in with our plans, provided it didn't cost them any more. There were financial implications for the climbing team as well; every day we were in the country was costing the team $595. In effect this meant that every day we spent hanging around was reducing the time we could afford to spend on the mountain. Balanced against this was the fact that many of the climbers wanted to take advantage of the rare opportunity to see the *tsechu*, and as the clouds and rain continued to blot out the valley, indicating that the monsoon was not yet finished, a delay was probably not any great disadvantage.

Nevertheless the decision to stay extra days in Thimphu, right though it was, was taken by Maggie without consulting the climbers or the trekkers. This was an easy thing to happen; we were all dashing around the town doing this that and the other, and Maggie found herself taking the obvious decision on behalf of all of us whilst she happened to be at the tourism office. It was all right the first time it happened; few people noticed. I had a private word with her, pointing out the implications and asking her not to take decisions without consultation, but then the next day, in an almost identical situation, Maggie, caught up in a whirlwind of arrangements for her trekkers, made the decision that we would all stay for the festival. Upon hearing this some of the climbers, particularly Steve Monks and Harry McAulay, were annoyed that the problems of delay had not been discussed with ourselves or the trekkers. This was aggravated by the fact that the film gear was now on its way, making it possible to leave the day before the festival.

We held a meeting at which everyone openly put their point of view. The conclusion was not so much that staying for one day of the festival was the wrong thing to do, but more that Maggie should not have taken a unilateral decision without first discussing the problem in a democratic way. Maggie had believed sincerely that she had been doing what everyone would be pleased with, and apologised for obeying her intuition. She had not thought that it would lead to any trouble. Above all else I wanted nothing to interfere with our having the happiest trip any of us had ever experienced, and felt that at all costs rows and frictions should not be allowed to develop. We all agreed that I, Allen Jewhurst (the film director) and Maggie would discuss issues affecting our three groups, having first talked them over with the members themselves.

The incident was undoubtedly a good thing to have happened as it pulled us all closer together. It focused our minds on avoiding situations of conflict, and from then on we operated in a way where each of us discussed our worries in an atmosphere of genuine co-operation. Allen went further, and promised that if we lost any days on the mountain as a result of staying for filming the *tsechu* he would pay for them out of his contingency money.

Beyond the problems of leaving, and the minor fact that I was finding it impossible to phone in the reports I had promised to BBC Radio in London, as the connecting operator in Calcutta would never answer the telephone, we were, in fact, all thoroughly enjoying ourselves. The large, rambling hotel was sumptuous by climbers' standards, and we were finding Bhutanese food very much to our liking. Rich spicy sauces, strange but tasty mushrooms from the forest, vegetables we had never seen before, hot chillies, yak cheese and red rice which had a slightly nutty flavour were all complemented by delicious meats. We had thought that since the Buddhist religion teaches against the taking of life there would be no meat in Bhutan, and it was some surprise to find plentiful fried pork and roast beef. The Bhutanese view is that as long as someone else has killed the meat it is all right to eat it; a special sect carries out the slaughtering, though whether they are Buddhist or not I couldn't discover. Their alternative to slaughter is to graze their animals close to a cliff edge in the hope that one or two of them will fall over of their own accord.

The tourist season had not arrived, and we virtually had the hotel to ourselves; one of the only guests happened to be Sir Edmund Hillary, who along with Tenzing Norgay was the first man to stand on the top of Everest. A nice coincidence, as the leader of the 1953 expedition, Lord John Hunt, was one of our patrons. Sir Edmund was in the country as New Zealand's High Commissioner to India, Nepal and Bhutan. Another coincidence was the fact that we had a New Zealand climber in our team, Lydia Bradey. I couldn't help thinking that perhaps fate had already decided that Lydia and Yeshey would be the first to stand on top of Bhutan's highest mountain, as a repeat of the 1953 Everest formula.

Jeremy Knight-Adams turned up at last. A plane had finally got through, but he came in for a lot of leg-pulling for missing the London flight. We presented him with a cardboard replica of an

41

alarm clock in the hope that it might remind him to keep up with us for the rest of the trip.

The hospitality of our hosts was remarkable. Every morning cars would arrive to pick us up to take us sightseeing. On one occasion a handful of us were taken by minibus to see the Queen Mother's palace; however, at the first bend in the road from where the roof of the palace could be seen the bus stopped and our guide explained that he dare not take us any further as we might offend Her Majesty. We did have freedom to go anywhere else we pleased, including the Tashichhodzong, though women are not allowed to stay there after 7 p.m., for the obvious reason that the monk body is celibate.

The day before the festival three of us bought *khos*, the traditional men's costume. They are very comfortable, but require a lot of practice to put on correctly. I took to wearing mine wherever I went and found that men and women alike frequently approached me, pulling at the pleats, and adjusting the belt to ensure that I looked properly dressed; usually they would also offer me betel nut to chew, a standard greeting. If one enters a dzong then a *comni* also has to be worn as a sign of respect to the religion; this even applies to the king. It is a white tasselled cotton scarf which is wrapped round one shoulder and looped down to just above the knee. Only the king and the Jey Khempo wear the saffron *comni*, and *dashos* (equivalent to lords) are recognised by an orange version, together with a short sword in a silver scabbard. It is not uncommon in Thimphu to see *dashos*, complete with sword, walking through the streets.

In the evening before the festival our hosts laid on a special meal for us, and the Chief Justice, 'Bengy', gave us a lecture with slides about black-necked cranes. These rare birds migrate between Tibet and one particular district in Bhutan. There are now only seven or eight hundred – which may be accounted for by the fact that the males look exactly like the females. An interesting thing is that before they take off on their migration a single bird flies ahead to check that there is no danger for the flock – perhaps a case of 'Time spent on reconnaissance is seldom wasted.'

As you might expect in a country that has had few Western visitors, Bhutan has quite a number of unique birds and animals, not only those creatures found at high altitude but also a wide variety in the steamy, tropical jungles of the south. The Bhutanese are conservationist-minded and in the south there is a wildlife reserve, the Manas Sanctuary. The park is the habitat of the golden langur, a monkey not in evidence anywhere else in the world. There are also elephants, tigers, wild buffalo, pygmy hog and the endangered great Indian rhino. Elsewhere such rare animals as the red panda, the musk deer and the takin can be found. The latter is a strange type of large deer. Its flesh is sometimes used as medicine and its horn is believed to have aphrodisiac qualities. We saw a small herd in the tiny zoo in Thimphu. Stranger animals are said to exist, like the thing that is a cross between an otter and a piglet which occasionally pops out of rivers; whenever it does there is supposedly a national calamity. Legend also has it that there is a giant conch-like creature which lives in a remote northern lake – the Bhutanese Loch Ness monster. At high altitudes there are snow leopards, blue sheep, ibex, tahr and even the occasional yeti.

I have read some very interesting accounts relating to the abominable snowman in Bhutan. A lot of the evidence was brought to light by Desmond Doig, a reporter with the *Daily Mail* in the late 1950s. He visited Bhutan in the days before it had roads and electricity, and talks extensively about an animal called a *dremo*, or *dredmo* (in Bhutan, *tremo*), or the blue bear of Tibet. He describes how this animal was discovered in 1853 by Edward Blyth, first Curator of the Asiatic Society, but that only six furs are known ever to have been in man's possession. Its habitat was supposed to have been Amdo, the Koko Nor region and the mountains of Kham in North-West China. In a Tibetan–English dictionary dated 1902 an entry for '*dredmo*' reads: 'though born a human being he has grown an impious savage . . . one who has gone astray from a religious life: a yellow bear: a species of bear'. Desmond Doig relates how he found one of the furs in a monastery in Bumthang: 'The name the Lama gave the animal was Dremo. According to him it had a human face and human feet. Quite obviously he was not trying to sell me the snowman. He was innocent of the outside world's interest in the Yeti, and the price he asked was not inspired.'

Unless there is journalistic licence in this report, it is believable, inasmuch as Bhutan at that time had no radio, no electricity, no roads and no foreigners (how Desmond Doig happened to be there I don't know). It would be extremely surprising if a lama in Bumthang had heard of the yeti. Doig also recounts a story of local men who, camped on a snowy ridge, had heard 'things' in the night:

They fanned up a dying fire and threw flaming brands at the unseen intruders. To their horror the brands were skilfully caught and thrown back at them. They would have fled but the night was as terrifying as their visitors, who were now whistling like traffic policemen. In the morning the snow was full of *Mi-Go* (snow-men) tracks.

Memoirs of a Mountaineer by F. Spencer Chapman gives more interesting stories, and again it is worth quoting:

Then he [a village headman] warned us about *Mi-Go* who were known to inhabit the northern valleys of Bhutan, and he told us a long story of some Phari traders who had lost their way on the Tremo La (the pass from Phari into Bhutan) in a snowstorm, and how they had seen the tracks of the snowmen and two of the party had disappeared in the night and had never been heard of since.

It is interesting to note that the Bhutanese created a set of stamps depicting the yeti, both male and female, though now they are rare collectors' items. I saw a set in the national museum in Paro. The stamps portray a stylised image of the creature, rather Neanderthal in appearance. The museum contains a complete display of Bhutan's unique stamps. Bhutan is known in philatelic circles to be the first country ever to have produced metal, silk and even three-dimensional stamps.

This idea that the yeti is a rather unusual and practically extinct bear sounds quite plausible to me. I have myself had encounters with brown bears on two previous Himalayan trips high above the snow line, and it is certainly not unheard of for bears to enter a climbing expedition's base camp in search of food. I heard of one Japanese expedition whose supplies of whisky were also consumed by the visiting bear! Brown bears are definitely commonplace in Bhutan and the locals have a healthy respect for them. We heard a couple of accounts of postmen being attacked as they travelled on foot between villages. Of course such an incident would only happen if you were to come upon a bear and surprise him, or bump into a female with a cub.

The Himalaya is such a vast range of complex, inaccessible mountains, uninhabited in the main, that it is easy to see how one rare animal might well go undetected for a long period of time, particularly in somewhere like Bhutan, which has had only a handful of expeditions. Not that we held out any hopes of seeing anything – our vast cavalcade would likely scare away anything in its path.

On 13 September, the day of the Thimphu *tsechu*, we awoke to a clear sky and in small groups we walked to the dzong. Most of the town was making its way there, all work in the capital having stopped. The people were dressed in their best clothes and jewellery, laughing and smiling in the sunshine. It appeared that the majority of the younger women had babies, which they carried on their backs, tucked into hand-woven shawls. We joined the throng walking under the weeping willows that form an avenue to the main gate of the dzong. Its stout stone pillars were bedecked with yellow, red, green and blue silk hangings. Jeff and I in our red tartan *khos* attracted considerable mirth, whether because of our appearance or Jeff's extrovert cavortings I wasn't certain. A hundred yards ahead the Tashichhodzong towered up in front of us, its white painted walls tapering, emphasising its size and creating an impression of power and age.

Tashichhodzong means 'Fortress of the Glorious Religion' and it dates back to the thirteenth century, when a monastery stood on the site. Over the intervening millenia it was enlarged, and suffered many times from earthquakes and fire. After Thimphu became the permanent capital in 1955, the late king, Jigme Dorje Wangchuck, decided to rebuild the dzong, already in a shaky condition, and work started in 1961. No plans were used, and it is built completely of traditional materials; there is not a nail in the whole building. The inner temples are original, and the workmanship of the new is of such excellent quality that it is virtually impossible to detect the difference.

A large crowd had gathered outside the main entrance, where soldiers in blue serge uniform stood on duty with fixed bayonets. A wide flight of stone steps led to an open-fronted bay in the main wall. Inside this bay monks chanted in deep tones, beating out a slow, hypnotic dirge on drums which they hit with curved sticks. Clouds of incense filled the air. We jostled up a dark inner flight of wide stairs, with huge, frightening deities in relief on the walls, until we emerged into another bay. Its walls were painted with mandalas and intricately detailed scenes of Buddha's life. As we emerged in a crush of people out of the dark stairwell into the sunlight, we saw in front of us a crowd of thousands in the main courtyard. They were sitting on the ground, or pressed right up against the walls, watching the 'Black Hat' dancers twirling in the centre of the square. The experience was one of stepping backwards in time. The ancient ceremony was still performed not for tourism (we were virtually the only white people there) but for the beliefs of the people. The loud noise of the twelve-foot-long Tibetan horns, the rhythmic clash of cymbals and drums, the low chanting, the crowd in clothing which had not changed in centuries were breathtaking.

I felt slightly self-conscious, being one of the few Europeans among such a huge crowd of Bhutanese. I need not have worried; we were quite welcome. The film team were already set up towards the front of the crowd, fairly inconspicuous in such a large gathering. Friendly hands helped us through the mass of people to join them.

The twenty-one Black Hat dancers stamped the ground, twisted, spun in unison and beat narrow circular drums with strangely curved sticks, which they held aloft on wooden spindles. Each was dressed in a multi-coloured skirt of silk and brocade with a picture of a demon on the front. Short capes of heavier material, richly embroidered with geometric symbols, covered their chests and backs, and on their heads they wore tall, pointed hats, the flat brims of which were rimmed with black fur. One or two of the more resplendent dancers also had wings of gold protruding from their hats. On their drums and from their hats and arms flew gossamer-thin scarves of brightly coloured silks. On their feet they wore felt and leather boots, of red, black, and green, with slightly upturned toes. There was a unique quality to the cyclical movements of slow stamping and fast spinning, the dazzling colours, the sonorous blasts of horn music, which I found almost spellbinding.

I learnt that the belief is that they have the power to subdue evil spirits and bring to the ways of Buddha those beings who cannot be led by peaceful means. It was explained to me that they do this by external compassionate anger, whilst internally achieving a peaceful state of mind. In the ritual we watched, the dancers had first formed a mandala, or mystic geometric figure, by pounding the earth with their feet, and then they cut the demons into pieces by making sacred mystic gestures. As a result they had taken possession of the earth, and in order to further protect it they danced the 'step of the thunderbolt' to impress their power upon it. The 'Dance of the Twenty-One Black Hats' is, apparently, often used as a ground purification rite when building dzongs or chortens in order to take possession of the ground from malevolent beings living there.

Over to the right was a group of young monks, dressed in their maroon robes. *En masse* their closely cropped hair appeared unusual and with their uniform grins they seemed clones of one another. They sat on the steps of one of the inner temples or leant out of its windows. The two inner temples were square-built in the same style as the main fortress walls, and formed roughly two sides of the massive, stone-flagged, courtyard. They tapered and rose to over a hundred feet above the square. Each had a roof in three tiers, the largest painted red with the smaller upper roofs yellow, capped by large brass ornaments. There were large overhanging eaves with golden gargoyles at each corner. The roof being raised a little above the main structure, there was room also for large carved and brightly painted animals under the eaves – dragons, white tigers and griffins holding snakes in their mouths. Masses of people had found their way up through the temple and were sitting there, legs dangling, looking down on the square. People had also climbed the two of three small trees on the edge of the square for a better view of the proceedings.

It seems that no bit of woodwork goes unpainted in a dzong; on the pillars, door frames, lintels, windows and alcoves there were either curly clouds, stiff flowers, swastikas, tantric symbols or carvings of pot-bellied men, demons or legendary animals. At the base of some of the inner buildings were rows of small prayer wheels, set in recesses; as people passed by they gave them a twirl and murmured 'Om ne mani padme hum', the standard Buddhist prayer, which roughly translated means 'O jewel in the centre of the lotus flower'. Elsewhere amongst the crowd there were many people spinning their own hand-held prayer wheels, the revolving brass cylinders packed inside with parchment on which the same magic words are printed, each revolution sending the prayer across the world.

On the edges of the crowd there was a troupe of clowns, all with wooden masks coloured red or orange, and all dressed in chequered clothes. The clowns either sat and told stories to the people nearest them or practised their mischievous pranks on the dancers and audience alike. In the afternoon, after a rain shower, they went round kicking the puddles over anybody and everybody, with people kicking the water back at them, great peals of laughter echoing through the courtyard.

I sat for a long time on the edge of the square, mesmerised by the spectacle. So much of my time had been taken up with organisational details over the previous days and for once there was nothing for me to do or think about other than to take delight in the people around me. I must have had a permanent smile stitched to my face.

Different troupes of dancers came on throughout the day; many wore exquisitely carved wooden masks depicting stags, hunting hounds, elephants, bulls, or hideous monsters. One of the dances told a story of four princesses who were left at home while their four princes went to the wars. While the princes were away the clowns barged into the set pieces and tried to disrupt the dancing of the girls, only to be chased around the square by an old woman who hit them on the head with a big stick.

After lunch, and a bit of rain, the crowd had thinned enough to allow me to wander about the dzong. I decided to try to make my way up through an inner temple to take some photos from under the eaves. Before leaving England I had been cautioned that foreigners were not encouraged to enter monasteries, and it was with some nervousness that I climbed the steep wooden stairs that led up to the entrance. Some monks stood in the dark doorway and by gestures I asked if it was all right for me to continue. They broke into smiles and one of them, beckoning, led me inside. More steep and narrow stairs took me to the first floor, where there was a temple. I wandered in to find a family sitting near the window, small children running around and hiding behind the thick wooden pillars. The floor was bare polished wood; the gigantic planks must have been hewn out of whole tree-trunks. Around the walls were hundreds of miniature clay buddhas on rows of shelves, and in the centre, behind an altar, was a huge golden figure with several heads and hundreds of arms. On each of the hands was painted an eye. There were many offerings of money and food on the altar. Butter lamps and incense burnt. The ceiling was grimy with centuries of soot, and brocade-lined *thankas* (religious paintings) and religious murals covered the walls. I felt a sense of awe, and stood there trying to imagine the centuries of meditation that had taken place in this room. Was the magic I felt a product of the beauty of the place, or was there some benevolent power here? In all religions there are beliefs and rituals that seem ridiculous, based on superstition and embellished legend. My logical mind told me that much of the content of these ancient beliefs had to be make-believe, but at the heart of Buddhism the principles are based on such goodness that one begins to wonder about the rest. Certainly this temple, this festival had created a powerful impression; the problem was in sorting out what was real and what was not.

On the floor above was another temple in a similar style and just as beautiful – too dark to photograph though, and I carried on up to the roof. To get into the loft there was half a tree-trunk with steps carved in it, tall, steep and hanging over a deep stairwell. The roof was supported on massive beams, covered in dust and pigeon droppings, and from the eaves the view looked over the rest of the dzong and the country beyond. From below the music drifted up and the people looked like ants. I took a shot with my Pentax and discovered that like an idiot I had run out of film.

Back down again I let the tide of things happening take me here and there. First three old men posed with their prayer wheels, one of them pulling faces and laughing, knowing it was a great joke. The wooden handle of a large knife stuck out of the folds in his *kho*. I was beckoned into the living quarters of some monks, tall frugal rooms with mats for sleeping and little else. Then I bumped into Jeremy Knight-Adams and we gravitated towards a building from which more music was coming, and to which monks were drifting in twos and threes. Over a wall some boy monks were throwing apples, hoping to hit someone on the head, and then running off.

We went through a narrow arch and suddenly the crowds were left behind. Should we be here? No one seemed to mind, so we cautiously followed the monks into a large hall. There were scores of red-robed figures sitting cross-legged on cushions in rows, chanting. Some wore red felt hats with a crest like a Roman legionary's helmet. Others held upright narrow drums on spindles, and after each chant hit them with curved sticks. We could dimly make out the Jey Khempo sitting on a raised dais leading the prayers. We tucked ourselves away in one corner, trying to be as unobtrusive as possible, content to watch the inexplicable litany unfolding before our amazed eyes. At another end of the room there was a small crowd of monks being handed what looked like money, or meal tickets. One of them came near and we made to ask him what he was holding. Unfortunately, two or three came over to us and I could see that we were getting stony glances from one of the elder monks walking down the aisles in the ceremony. I felt it was time for us to leave.

Back in the main square we headed over to the central temple. We had already been told by our hosts that we were allowed to enter, provided we removed our shoes; the impurity of the dead skin of an animal would not be appropriate in the temple. Inside we discovered one of the largest statues I've ever seen. It rose, gilded, through two floors of the building and gazed down at us impassively. A monk sat mumbling low incantations, swaying back and forth, counting beads on a rosary, seemingly oblivious of our presence. I was so awestruck by the magnificence of my surroundings that I drifted slowly through the room like a sleep walker, afraid even to speak to Jeremy standing alongside.

Back in the square the final dance, depicting how the sage Milarepa tamed a stag and hounds, drew to a close and the last of the people drifted home. A few of us stayed to help the film crew with their equipment and play football with some children. The flocks of resident pigeons swooped down as a monk threw corn on the stone flags; the day of a lifetime was over.

6
The Road-Block Test

Several days before the *tsechu*, BTC had sent on ahead by truck all the provisions for Base Camp and the walk-in, all the expedition equipment, and some of the twelve Bhutanese staff who were to accompany us to the mountain. They were now waiting at Jakar, the last village in the Bumthang valley. The radio also conveyed the message that sixty-one horses had arrived from surrounding villages and were corralled outside the hotel. Their owners were showing signs of impatience. The film gear arrived from Calcutta, and on 14 September we boarded two minibuses and a blue pick-up and climbed out of Thimphu, past Simtoka Dzong, and up the steep, twisting mountain road towards the Dochu La, the first of many high passes on our journey east.

We had been warned that it would be a long day's drive, ten or twelve hours, all on mountain roads. I felt a schoolboy excitement again at the prospect of seeing some of the romantic places that up until now had just been strange names and historical annotations on a crumpled large-scale map I had found in the depths of the Royal Geographical Society's map room. I had hoped for a glimpse of the old capital, Punakha, besides seeing Wangdiphodrang, the Pele La, Tongsa Dzong, and the Black Mountains.

We came up through forests of cedar and rhododendron, thick with fine strands of hanging lichen, the air smelling sweetly in the early morning. It was misty and chilly, and on the top of the pass there was a chorten and many prayer flags on tall poles in a clearing. I noticed absently that the road did not pass to the left of the chorten, as is the usual custom. We cheered as we reached the crest, as we had just topped 10,000 feet.

On the other side the clouds gave us a break, and as we dropped down through the hairpins the forest spread out below us as far as the eye could see. It had an ethereal appearance, the mists hanging in the valleys and outlining the jungle-covered ridges. The sun shone, so I climbed out the window and on to the roof rack. This was not approved of by the driver, who no doubt had been cautioned not to cause an international incident by losing any of us, and when we stopped for a break Yeshey politely intimated that I was causing the driver unhappiness.

I went back and sat next to Ole Fink Larsen, the film researcher. Ole had been brought in at the last moment as part of the film crew as he knew something of Buddhism and was a good interviewer. He lives in America and his business is running a series of 'self-actualisation' courses. As far as I could make out these are intense weekends designed to bring about a better understanding of oneself and one's own potentials and what life is all about. That probably sounds cranky to an Englishman, but Ole's sincerity was unquestionable and it is a fact that although Dutch by birth he smiled so much that his face bore a closer resemblance to a Tibetan's.

Down and down we went, through gorges with fast-flowing rivers, over forested ridges, along the road clinging to the sides of cliffs, until we came to a wide valley. Houses like Alpine log chalets started to appear on terraced hillsides and we followed the Sankosh river towards Wangdiphodrang. A large, important dzong stood on a rocky hill, overlooking the river. It was built in 1638 by the Shabdung, Nawang Namgyal, and legend has it that in a dream he was told that if a dzong was built in the shape of a sleeping bull peace would come to the country. The site was chosen when four crows were seen flying away in four directions. This was thought an auspicious sign, signifying the spread of religion from that place in all four directions.

The penlop at Wangdiphodrang Dzong used to be the third most important chieftain in the kingdom, after those of Tongsa and Paro, excluding the two heads of state, particularly as the dzong was so close to the old capital, Punakha. Until 1968 there was a beautiful cantilevered bridge here, built three hundred years ago, but it was swept away by floods and unfortunately has been replaced by a Bailey bridge.

Just behind the fortress is a small township where we stopped briefly. I little imagined that I was to see a good deal more of it later in the day. We carried on up the steep valley of the Tang Chu, heading towards the Pele La, at just over 11,000ft the highest pass we were to cross by road. Soon we were back in the forest and an hour after leaving Wangdi' we came to a section where a landslide had obviously recently taken the road away; all that was there was a muddy, rutted section on an incline. The driver charged at it and, with us giving the vehicle considerable vocal encouragement and bouncing up and down in the rear, the bus just made it. A mile further on there was a section of road literally carved out of the side of a cliff, with a very long drop below. The driver was much more cautious on this section, which was just as well because on rounding a corner we found ourselves confronted with a massive road-block.

A section of the cliff had collapsed, leaving hundreds of tons of rock – boulders the size of bungalows – blocking our way. In that instant of seeing an impossible obstacle on the only road in the country I knew that there *had* to be a solution, but my spirits fell at the thought of trying to organise a gang with dynamite to open a way for us. I had visions of being stuck for another three or four days. The delay in Thimphu had been barely acceptable to our programme, but this was now a serious situation.

Everybody got out and sauntered over. There was a jeep on the other side and we learnt from the driver that the collapse had happened only ten minutes earlier. He could testify to this as he had just been along the road in the other direction. The remains of the cliff still looked decidedly tottery up above. Would any more rocks come down? The film crew were frantically unloading their gear, whilst I tried to work out what the alternatives were. Where was the nearest telephone? Who was the man in charge of road repairs? Who in the capital would authorise the work? Could we get transport from the other side to pick us up? How long did we think it would take to clear the road? Was it worth going back to Wangdi' or should we try to borrow the jeep and go forwards to Tongsa? When would it stop raining?

The discussion ebbed and flowed, people milled around, ideas were thrown into the air only to fall back on stony ground, cameras clicked, a mike was pinned to my chest. It was acting time again. 'OK, BBC TV news, roll 32, road-block Bhutan, Take one. When you're ready, Steve . . .'

I couldn't help laughing to myself – a classic adventure scene, another test entitled 'How to deal with a road-block on a mountain road'. It's the sort of event every Himalayan expedition is supposed to have.

The man with the jeep took us completely by surprise when he told us that the Indian army officer in charge of road repairs had a camp up near the Pele La, a ten-minute drive on the other side of the rockfall. What a stroke of luck! In a 200km stretch of road the right man was on the doorstep. Jeremy Knight-Adams, Peter Godwin (the *Sunday Times* reporter), Singey Wangchuck and I persuaded the jeep driver to take us up there. We arrived at the camp to find an Indian captain and his adjutant sitting in an army lorry dishing out money to the Indian roadworkers. It was pay day. Each man received his bundle of rupees and put his thumbprint in a large book. Patience is everything in the East and we had to wait for some time.

The Indian army officer did not seem much interested in our plight. It was not clear whether he had the authority to do anything. We had already made up our minds that even if he did something it would not happen fast enough. We asked him if we could borrow some transport to go to Tongsa to arrange for our own lorry to come back from Bumthang to pick us up. No, this was not possible, but if we waited he would come and look at the problem. Nobody seemed to know whether there was a telephone at Wangdi', but there was probably a radio; there was certainly a phone at Tongsa but no way to get there. We decided to go back to Wangdi', arrange accommodation for us all, and try to get through to Karchung Wangchuck in Thimphu, who would be able to radio Bumthang for our lorry. Meanwhile, crates marked 'Danger – Explosives' were being thrown in the back of an army lorry, and soon we were back at the road-block.

At that time it did not seem remotely conceivable that the rock could be shifted and the road rebuilt in anything less that two or three days, so Yeshey and I took the blue pick-up and headed for Wangdi'. Once there we found the radio operator and discovered that there was a telephone. It worked after a fashion, but Yeshey held no confidence that his message for Karchung, repeated several times at increasing volumes, had actually been understood, and so the man opened the radio office and started the generator and we tried again. The room had three sets of radio gear: an enormous pile of Westinghouse equipment with 'US Army' stamped on it, a medium-sized set of British origin, and a tiny Japanese set with an old Morse code key. The Japanese set worked, but again Karchung could not be found.

Above *Leaping dancer making mystic gestures to quell bad spirits, Thimphu tsechu. (Photo: Steven Berry)*

Below *Clowns 'molesting' two princesses in the Dance of the Four Noblewomen, Thimphu tsechu. (Photo: Harry McAulay)*

Overleaf *A hermit's nest high on a cliff in Paro valley. (Photo: John Knowles)*

Although there are telephones in a few of the larger townships, radio is still used as the main communication outside Thimphu and Paro, particularly for the east of the country, and a radio operator enjoys quite a high status in his community.

It was not raining at Wangdi'; in fact, it was quite hot and, as we had to wait for an hour for Karchung to radio back, we took some shade in a tea shop. Posters of Indian film stars and newspaper cuttings were pasted on the walls, which were otherwise painted in light-green gloss. The rudimentary tables were topped in formica, and a couple of healthy-looking mastiffs lay asleep on the dusty floor. The place was not the Ritz, but it was clean. Yeshey ordered some *mo mos* – minced meat and chilli in soft pastry – and sweetly sugared tea for the two of us.

The normal diet for country people is rice, often mashed up and rolled into balls, eaten with perhaps dried meat – pork or beef usually, sometimes yak – and all sorts of vegetables. Everything contains chillies to the power of ten; how they eat their food without bursting into flames defeats me. Chillies are dried on any available rooftop, and when we came down off the 'hill' all the roofs burned red with the fresh harvest. Bhutanese are also very fond of yak cheese, which may be cooked in a sauce, or, in their favourite form, *churpi*, dried into small rock-solid squares and then sucked and chewed on, rather like sweets. These squares of cheese are set on a piece of string and often hang round people's necks.

As far as drink is concerned butter tea, Tibetan-style, is usual and it is rude to refuse a second cup if offered. The offering of a second cup means that you are accepted as a friend. It bears scant resemblance to English tea, and is made from solid bricks, imported from China via India, with butter and salt added. It is, as they say, an acquired taste. Village people also drink *chhang*, a rice beer, and *arra*, which is a clear spirit, distilled from rice, maize, wheat, or barley. The latter does not taste strongly of alcohol but five minutes after a couple of cupfuls one notices the effect.

There were quite a few people in the tea house, greatly outnumbered by flies, and, like most Bhutanese, they derived great amusement from looking through the zoom lens on my camera. They also offered the usual practical advice on how to dress properly in a *kho*. The village schoolteacher was there, a New Zealander called Richard. He worked for VSO, a British aid organisation. I had a long chat with him and came to realise that he was living on a starvation diet – that is to say, he had no one to talk to. I liked him and admired what he was doing. Could a man like him ever live a sane ordinary life in the West after teaching schoolchildren in the back of beyond?

We kept trying with the radio, and discovered that our truck had left Bumthang a couple of days earlier, travelling in the opposite direction towards India. However, Karchung was trying to organise another one. We booked everyone into the 'tourist' bungalow and ordered an evening meal for twenty-two people; the others were supposed to follow us down after watching the progress on the road. Time went by but they didn't arrive. At 7.30 p.m. we saw the lights of a vehicle coming back down the valley. It proved to be a car from Tongsa! The army had blasted a way through and rebuilt the road in six hours; our party had got through and travelled on without us! I told the tea shop owner to dish the food out to anybody in the village who wanted it, and we set off in pursuit.

I would have felt safe if I had been driving myself, but we still had nine hours to go, in the dark, with a driver who must surely have been in training for the Monte Carlo rally. We had picked up a young American in Wangdi' and it was now a little squashed on the bench seat of the pick-up. We came to where the road-block had been. Most of the debris was still there, but somehow a gap had been created just wide enough to get a vehicle through. We inched our way along, the wheels on the very edge of the drop. I held the door-handle with the vain thought that I would jump if the road collapsed.

We drove into the night. We talked, dozed on each other's shoulders, endured periods of silence, and dozed again. How could this man stay awake behind the wheel? I found myself jerking awake every time we went round a particularly bad bend, expecting the worst. I fought as hard as I could to stay awake. Towards the end of the nine hours on mountain roads both the American and I were having hallucinations; I distinctly remember seeing us driving down a straight bit of road, following the tail lights of another car and I received a severe mental shock when we went round a sharp corner that had not existed in my vision.

The blue pick-up finally ground to a halt in Bumthang at 4.30 a.m. We'd been up since 6.15 a.m. the previous day – twenty-two hours. I was miserable with tiredness, a piece of human jetsam. I even fell asleep leaning on the bonnet while someone knocked up the manager of the hotel. The driver was still smiling.

I was woken at 10 a.m. to be told that the horses had tired of waiting for us and had dispersed to their various villages. They would be back tomorrow. I doubt whether anyone would have persuaded me to move very far that day in any case. Everyone had gone off to watch a festival in the local village. I couldn't face it; my body demanded more rest. Having gathered the situation report, I flaked out again.

The hotel we were in was a group of single-storey thatched chalets, surrounded by orchards, with a larger central building housing the open-plan restaurant, bar and large sitting room. Newly built, but all in superb Bhutanese style. That first evening we had as our guests Yoshiro Imaeda and his French wife, Françoise. This was another piece of the jigsaw fitting into place, as they were authors of a coffee-table book full of wonderful photographs which I had used extensively to sell the expedition to sponsors. I had found the book by accident when, wandering round the Portobello Road, I had walked into a book shop, The Travel Bookshop, to discover inside an exhibition of photographs taken from it. It turned out to be the best £19.50 I had ever invested. Yoshiro and Françoise both now live in Bhutan. Françoise is currently working on an official history of the country, and funnily enough had been working in BTC at the time I made the climbing application.

The atmosphere here was different from western Bhutan. In Thimphu there was bustle, cars, a telex machine, government in progress, cinemas and cake shops. In Bumthang there was rural peace and quiet – just the road going on east towards Mongar, Tashigang, Samdrup Jonghar and India. It is a beautiful place with its scattered villages, orchards, wild peach trees, winding river and many monasteries and temples. Just across the valley, on the spur of a hill, the Jakar Dzong, or 'Castle of the White Bird', stood waiting to be visited, but there was not enough time.

After lunch we went up to the village for the festival. It was held in the main square, of which an eighth-century temple formed one side and rough village houses formed the others. On the roof of the temple stood two monks blasting away on long Tibetan horns; later on there were monks with red pointed hats blowing brass and silver trumpets, a much shriller, reedy sound. To one side was erected a temporary stage, draped in silk hangings, where the head lama sat, a jovial, benign-looking man in gold robes and an ornate, pointed gold hat. He sat there chanting and occasionally ringing a handbell.

Most of the villagers were sitting or milling around in the square, feeding children, drinking, laughing, catching up on gossip no doubt, and generally enjoying themselves. Behind the stage there was an area out of sight of the lama where worldly vice was in progress; there was a darts match with large amounts of money being gambled on the winner, men laughing and playing good-naturedly at pulling the money out of each other's hands. Darts takes on a new perspective in Bhutan. The target is just a small upright piece of wood in the ground, and the darts are about a foot long. They are made from a fairly heavy boss of wood with some chicken feathers sticking out of one end and a nail in the other. The dart is thrown with all one's might from a distance of about fifty feet. Closest to the target is the winner. Bhutanese have an irrepressible sense of good fun, and each throw would be accompanied by whoops, shouting and dancing up and down. A card game was in progress as well; Jeff and John Knowles (elder statesman of the trekkers) won some money, I believe. Large volumes of *chang* and *arra* were being consumed by all.

The clowns with their grotesque wooden masks were there, amusing everybody with their antics, and traditional dancing had taken place in the morning. The main event was yet to come, however – the blessing of the villagers by the head lama.

Things gradually started to happen. The monks with the trumpets emerged from the temple and slowly walked amongst the crowd, their instruments hung with white silk scarves. The village headman and his family arrived and were ushered to the best stall cushions near the stage. The headman wore his red *comni* with white stripes, denoting his rank. After a little while a group of older monks appeared and circulated amongst the people. Some poured holy water into outstretched hands, others threw millet over everybody, and others handed out thin strips of coloured cotton. The cotton is tied round the neck to ward off evil spirits, and its effectiveness lasts until it breaks.

Eventually the head lama left the stage and, with monks in front making a way for him, he walked up and down, placing a strange-looking gold vase on top of each person's head and murmuring his blessing. The people covered their mouths and noses with their hands as they bowed before him – I presumed so that he would not have to breathe their impure air. He was a kind-looking man, and as people surged forwards, reaching to touch him if nothing else, he smiled benignly at them as though they were all his errant children.

The day I was in Wangdi' I had met an English girl, a friend of the schoolteacher, and she told me of a strange experience she had had at a blessing. She first explained that she was a born sceptic in all religious matters and when she was encouraged to accept the blessing by some local women at a festival she had rather scorned the idea, but had done it anyway, more out of politeness than anything else. The lama had put his hands on her head and she had felt, as she described, a 'warmth' flowing through her, and for at least a week afterwards she had felt much more relaxed than usual.

At the lama passed close to me I leant forward and he gave me his blessing, but I can't say I felt anything unusual.

Eventually it was time to leave and we drifted out of the village. Out on the track we came upon a family who were in hysterics, as the husband had had so much to drink that he could no longer walk, and his wife and children were pulling at him, trying to carry him home, without much success. We also passed an elderly couple, both rather merry, arms round each other like young lovers, a picture of carefree happiness.

The best of the day was yet to come. After the usual delicious evening meal a bonfire was lit in a field next to the hotel, the Glenfiddich whisky was broken out and we started our own party. Yeshey had by now introduced us to all our trekking staff, and it was not long before they were singing Bhutanese songs to us, and we were replying with old Beatles tunes. Steve Monks had brought with him a couple of small speakers for his Sony Walkman and we danced on the grass. What made the evening so special, though, was the arrival of quite a large group of village women, who came to sing and dance for us. Today I don't know whether it was completely impromptu or whether Yeshey had it organised, but in any event it was a wonderful open gesture of friendship.

They formed a circle near the fire, the twentieth century was turned off, and the sweet plaintive songs taught to them by their mothers, and their mothers before them, seemed to me to speak of the beauty of their life in this incredible land. Sad love songs were followed by the nearest thing they have to rock and roll, and we all joined hands and danced round the blazing fire together, getting faster and faster, all of us laughing with no barriers, just simple friendship.

7

The Hot Springs at Dur Sachu

My research had shown that there were no detailed maps of the area we were to walk through, and that no British people had explored the Mangde Chu valley which was to lead us to Base Camp. There was a sketch map in the 1985 Japanese report showing ridges and rivers and a few place-names, and we were not likely to get lost like the Americans, since Yeshey had previously been to Base Camp. We could hardly claim, therefore, that we were heading into completely virgin territory, but nevertheless I for one had been looking forward to this part of the trip as much as anything else. There is something about the idea of entering virtually unknown country that generates in me a wild excitement.

In my imagination I had thought that there would be a few villages before we left the lower lands behind, and that once we were out of the valleys we would leave the cloud and rain behind as well. Neither was true. Once we had left Bumthang the only signs of habitation were a few yak herders' huts, used as temporary refuge in the summer months. During nine days of walking we met just a handful of people, usually yak-herding folk. On the first day we encountered a party of villagers who had been to the hot springs at Dur Sachu. We exchanged the traditional greeting of 'Kuzo zompo la', and they replied with a bow, their hands held together, showing their respect. We were a source of great amusement to them, in our strange Western clothes, with rucksacks on our backs and cameras around our necks. Their childlike happiness was such a far remove from the rush and sophistication of the twentieth century, and such a pleasure to behold. Although these people lived a life we could not possibly understand in any depth, we could still laugh and joke with them. My only hope was that they did not look at us and envy our material possessions. Their life was obviously hard, and I could imagine that in their naivety they might have thought our Western gadgetry could bring a better life. Undoubtedly they need modern medicine, but I felt sure they would be better off without the rest.

The first three days would see us to the hot springs, where we were due to change the sixty-one horses for yaks. This had been organised ahead of our arrival, but we knew that delay was possible. The system is that BTC makes a request to the Home Office, which in turn makes a request to the district administrator, who in turn contacts the nearest village headman, who tries to get the yaks to the right place at the right time. In fact in our experience, considering the potential pitfalls, the system works remarkably well.

From what I could make out some yak men are not too keen on the idea of foreign expeditions climbing the high peaks. They see the mountains as gods who should not be angered. There was even a deputation sent to the National Assembly one year to make a complaint, saying more of their yaks were dying of illness than was usual, because the mountain gods were being angered. The king himself convinced the deputation that tourism was for the good of everyone; certainly we encountered absolutely no ill feeling towards us. Our yak men were not slow to realise that they had a monopoly of supply and, since the first Japanese expedition, they had been putting up their prices for porterage to their own government employers.

We started the march-in on 16 September, the idea being to arrive at the mountain at the very end of the monsoon. A study of an atlas had shown that Bhutan catches the worst part of the Indian monsoon, its effect lessening the further west one goes along the main Himalayan chain. The only other information we had to work on was the experience of the Japanese, and reports of various people who had been in, or near, Bhutan at that time of year. The best of this information was some climatic tables produced by Drs M. Ward and F. Jackson from their 1965 trek in the Lunana region, a little to the west of us. These two British doctors, and a colleague, Dr Aubrey Leatham (who had personally helped our expedition), were physicians to the late king, who gave Ward and Jackson permission to trek through Lunana. Both men are keen climbers, Michael Ward having been expedition doctor on the 1953 expedition to Everest. During their trek they took the opportunity to make ascents of Peak St George, 17,850ft, Yak Peak, 18,000ft,

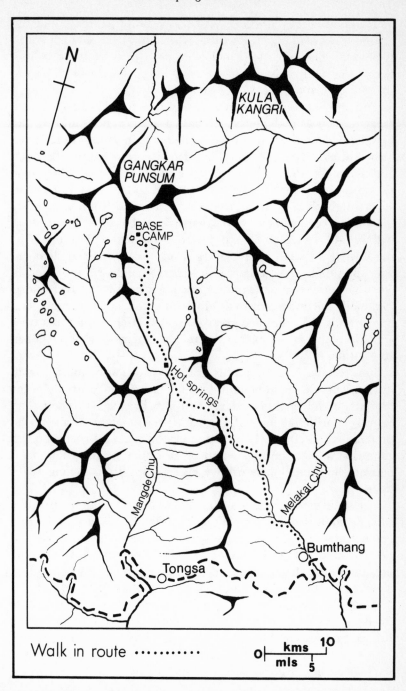

Walk in route ···········

and Gangto Peak, 18,000ft, and from the latter they obtained distant views of Gangkar Punsum, which they believed to be called Rinchitta. The mountain had been seen at least twice before, perhaps even as early as 1865, and its height fixed from a pass to the east by Captain H. C. R. Meade in 1922.

The weather could have treated us worse, for although it rained every day it was really heavy on only a few occasions and we had to walk through sleet only twice. Usually the mornings were in fact quite sunny. Mist and cloud swirled around continually, often adding an air of mystery to the lakes and high passes. The jungle that enclosed us for the first two days was sodden and humid, but surprisingly there were no leeches. We hopped from one muddy boulder to the next on a narrow marshy path beside a river studded with rapids. Thick bamboo, pine and cedar hemmed us in, and as the altitude increased so the layers of vegetation changed. To begin with the jungle was so dank that the tree-trunks were covered in thick, wet mosses and the undergrowth was a wall of lush greenery. Gradually the undergrowth thinned, and branches were hung with fine strands of lichen, like green cobwebs. Higher still birch trees appeared, and at the end of the tree line acres of rhododendron covered the hillsides.

Steve Findlay, our food officer and expedition botanist, was in his element and could be found round each fresh corner up to his armpits in foliage, doing research for Bristol University and happily chortling to himself. Steve is a keen amateur botanist, who prefers orchids to nearly anything else in the world, and he was ecstatic at walking through an area where other humans of his kind had not had the chance to give every living thing a long Latin name.

The days were long and arduous, and at the end of the first day Maggie confessed her worry to me that Tan had lagged far behind and had found the distance too great. She was exhausted. We had risen from 8,400ft at Bumthang to 10,000ft, a point at which some people feel the effects of altitude in the form of headaches and, in Tan's case, slight nausea and a loss of appetite. Our expedition doctor, Ginette Harrison, was a specialist in high-altitude medicine, having taken part in research expeditions in Nepal, Kenya, and Alaska. She had stayed with Tan most of the day and felt that perhaps the first day had been a shock to her system, and that as yet there was nothing to worry about.

Every evening we gathered together to eat in the main mess tent, and never have I experienced such a level of friendship amongst a group of people who were just thrown together. As climbers we had originally been a little dubious about taking along a bunch of people we didn't know, and we had imagined that all sorts of problems would occur. However, amongst such a large group there was no one who jarred, no one who got on people's nerves, and no one who complained. Even when we hit an all-time low in terms of hardship, the night at the yak herders' camp a day before Base Camp, there was an unspoken single-mindedness of purpose that made us all pull together. They were people from all callings, living all sorts of complicated lives, but in each and every case the same determination to make it to Base Camp and see us started on the mountain swept aside all differences.

The evenings in the mess tent were always a party, and after each meal the cook, Phuntso, brought in a bottle of local whisky, thoughtfully provided by BTC, and labelled 'Army Welfare Project, Gayleghug Distillery'. We also had with us two crates of Glenfiddich; by the time we arrived at Base Camp we had one bottle left. Jeff sometimes produced his mandolin and mouth-organ; we sang, we played games, but more than anything we laughed.

There were problems, of course. The first was that Ole had a tight schedule and it was looking more and more as though he would not have the time to come all the way to Base Camp. Yeshey wanted to send him back from the hot springs with the horses; Alan wanted him to come on further with us as Ole hadn't yet interviewed the climbers for the film.

Unless people take up completely inflexible positions, problems like this are easily solved, and I found Alan to be a master of compromise. He is a film man first and foremost but has been on several big expeditions and has many climbing friends. His equipment seemed to comprise a collection of things he had been given, or inherited, from previous trips – Joe Tasker's gloves, Pete Boardman's helmet, Don Whillan's down suit, and so on. He understands climbers and their mentality perfectly; he is at heart one himself, and instead of there being an 'us and them' feeling it was like just having a few more friends along. Some sequences had to be staged, but there was no question of performing boring rehearsals or doing several takes; we became oblivious of the ever-present camera and clapper-board, even though we were aware that the film was costing £140,000.

The end of the second day saw us leave the jungle, and after a steep pull and a long traverse round a mountainside we entered a high valley with a languid river and a few yak herders' huts. Cloud covered all the peaks which ringed the valley, making it look like a dead end. It was a gloomy place, and when I arrived it was raining.

I walked into the first hut to get away from the rain. It was very basic – low built, four walls of rough stone, no windows, no door, and just some rough-hewn planks for a roof. Inside practically everything seemed black with soot. Acrid smoke stung my eyes from the wood fire on which some large pans of water were being heated. Dried yak meat hung from the rafters, as did anything else that could not find a place on the bare earth floor. A group of Bhutanese yak men crouched round the fire, some with bare feet and dressed in rough yak-hair *khos*, their narrow eyes screwed up against the smoke. The room was thick with fumes, whose only escape was the holes in the roof. My eyes just could not tolerate the painful stinging and I hovered in the open doorway. Our horses had arrived and loads were being dumped unceremoniously in the mud. There was a large group of yaks in the valley and I watched as they were slowly rounded up and tethered for the night.

Born to withstand the rigours of living at high altitude, they are massive animals, much larger than a bull, with very thick furry coats and impressive horns. They are irascible in nature and even their handlers treat them with the utmost caution. On one of the early British diplomatic missions to Bhutan in 1783, led by Samuel Turner, two yaks were sent back to England. One survived the journey and Turner had this to say about the animal:

This, which was a bull, remained for some time after he landed in a torpid, languid state . . . soured by the impatient and injudicious treatment of his attendants, during the long voyage, it soon became dangerous to suffer this bull to range at liberty abroad. He had at all times been observed to bear a marked hostility towards horses; and . . . he happened to gore a valuable coach horse belonging to Mr. Hastings, which had the range of the same pasture with him, and, lacerating the entrails, occasioned his death.

As I watched the herd of about thirty gathering, the horses keeping a respectful distance, I noticed that there was one which seemed larger than the rest standing in the middle of the others, snorting. It really was the most unusual noise; the whole body seemed to be used as a bellows and the result was a rhythmic blowing sound. One of the other yaks moved forwards and challenged him by returning the snorts. Suddenly they charged at each other and the power of the impact as they crashed head-on should have knocked them both out. They charged several times before the challenger backed off, looking groggy. Our Bhutanese horsemen raised a cheer and the large yak stood snorting aggressively, while the others wisely gave him plenty of room.

On another day our group of yaks were slowly climbing up a hillside to the constant shouting, whistling, and occasional stone-throw of the herders when another large group appeared coming down towards us. Both groups stopped and started snorting; our yaks had their tongues comically lolling out from the effort of climbing the mountainside. Both sets of herders moved into top gear to avoid a full-scale battle and eventually the two groups were steered well apart. I was left with the impression that these animals are really just wild, that man and his loads on their backs are like ticks, something that has to be tolerated, and that the yaks just don't have the wit to throw off man's yoke.

On that second night we heard that four of the horses had bolted in the morning and several of our loads had been temporarily left behind. Peter Santamera's sleeping bag and the medical box were part of this kit. Such was the confusion that in any case it had become impossible to find anything in the darkness and the rain, with a hundred loads lying around in the mud. Peter was a marine engineer when he was not converting cottages in the Lake District. A tough, wiry man, he endured a cold night, sleeping in a one-piece down suit. Later, not content with reaching Base Camp, he carried loads across the glacier and made it with us to Advance Base Camp at 18,000ft.

Far worse on that second night was Tan, who had had a gruelling day of ten and a half hours and had gone straight to bed feeling all in. Ginette and Maggie had again stayed with her most of the day, and both were showing great concern that she had lost her appetite, and thought she might wish to turn back. I went to see her.

Tan was of that breed of British person who, once decided on something, saw it through no matter what. All her energy was thrown behind whatever she did. Once a genuine friend, always a friend – but woe betide anyone who got on the wrong side of her. Unimpeachable values – someone you could always trust.

I knew how hard this would be for her but she showed none of it, telling me not to worry, that she would have a rest day or wait and return to Thimphu with Ole on his return from the hot springs at Dur Sachu. In the event, the next day Tan decided to carry on. We had at least been told by our guides that the third day would be shorter, if a little steeper, and we could expect a march of only six hours. Their memory of the route turned out to be wrong; it was the hardest march so far. Tan had another terrible day, but sensibly for the last part she requisitioned a horse.

The day dawned bright and sunny, and what a joy it was to be in the clear light and clean air of a remote mountain valley! We walked beside a slow-flowing river with a pair of white-capped river chats, and a hoopoe keeping us company. The latter is one of Bhutan's commonest birds, pretty and brown-striped, with a long bill and an erectile crest. Rocky peaks, free of cloud for once, towered above us on both sides. We knew there was a large pass to cross today, the Jule La, at 14,500ft, and before long we started the long haul out of the bottom of the valley. We climbed past a pretty waterfall and through a stratum of rock peppered with rough garnets. Below us a long line of people and horses were strung out, the large brightly coloured golf umbrellas and the alloy boxes strapped to the animals striking a discordant note on the remote hillside. The sounds of the horsemen whistling and cajoling their pack animals, the gentle wind in the rocks and the bells round the necks of the ponies were the only sounds to be heard.

Five hundred feet below the pass we came to a lake, where Steve Monks and Ginette had stripped off for a swim. It was a special place, unspoilt and peaceful. I found myself thinking about the hundreds of thousands of years that had gone by with no appreciable change, just the passing of seasons. Elsewhere in the world empires had risen and fallen, wars had been fought, cities and civilisations had come and gone, but this place had remained untouched. I felt humble sitting there watching the ripples on the lake, enjoying for my brief moment the peace that was invested in the place. Later on that day I was told the story of a nun who, on her way back from the hot springs, had slipped and fallen from a cliff overlooking the lake, and had drowned there, though our Bhutanese friends could not be sure when this had happened.

We made a brief stop for lunch at the Jule La, a rocky saddle with a few cairns and prayer flags. It had started to rain and we ran down the other side to a much larger lake, where some Bhutanese women were looking after their yaks. They were shy but, showing their friendship, offered us some yak curd, which they carried in bamboo tubs. Curiously, our own yaks seemed to like bathing, because they waded up to their necks along the edge of the lake, soaking many of our loads. We had been told that an hour and a half from the Jule La would see us at the hot springs, but after passing over another small pass, the Gokthong La, the path carried on down back into the jungle. Hours went by as the steep path zigzagged, becoming muddier and muddier, more and more tangled with tree roots, losing all the height it had taken us days of sweat to gain.

We dropped 4,000ft to Dur Sachu, a series of small, muddy, terraced clearings with a couple of huts amongst lush vegetation and forest. Exhausted though we were, we headed straight for the hot springs. They were wooden tubs, set into the ground, fed with hot sulphurous water straight out the mountainside, and right next to a noisy mountain stream. There was enough room in each tub for six or seven people. A rough wooden shelter kept off the rain. The air was hot and humid. Blissful torpor replaced our disgruntled feelings at having had twice as hard a day as we had anticipated. Shortly darkness came, and more of the others arrived. Soon there were naked people running from one tub to another, shouting. It seemed unreal, what with the steam and the sulphur, the noise of the river, the sounds of the forest. We could have been in Central Africa, not the Himalaya.

That night there seemed to be a general desire for a rest day. Yeshey was consulted. He felt that the trekkers would not be charged an extra day and in any case he seemed to be involved in protracted negotiations with the yak herders who had been at Dur Sachu for some time waiting for us. So we stayed. The sun shone and we relaxed, pottered around, read novels, were interviewed by Ole and enjoyed regular visits to the springs, where we sat or slept until we could take the heat no longer.

Tan had decided that Dur Sachu was the end of the trail for her; she would go back with Ole and Peter Godwin, the *Sunday Times* reporter. Nothing was said during dinner and after coffee was served there was an expectant silence. Everyone was waiting for me to express our feelings.

'Unaccustomed as I am to public speaking, and knowing I'll have the piss taken out of me if I get too carried away, I won't go on too long but I just want to say a few words about Tan. If if wasn't for her we wouldn't be here today . . .'

Tan interrupted: 'Yes you would, somebody else would have done it.'

'No they wouldn't. We owe it to you, Tan, and anyway I also want to say that I know that over the last few days you must have been having a great personal struggle, and there were probably times when you felt alone, but we were all rooting for you. I guess it's fate that you were only meant to get as far as the hot springs at Dur Sachu. In any case, I just want to thank you for all you have done for us and to say how sorry I am that you can't come all the way to Base Camp.'

Tan smiled and seemed composed. She started to reply but then all her feelings spilled over and she started crying. Maggie moved across and held her. It was right that we should share with her the pain – she had given us so much, she should not leave keeping the feelings inside herself. We were close friends. To cry was no shame; it was perfectly natural.

Above   *Loading the 71 horses at the start of the march-in. (Photo: Steven Berry)*

Below   *Yaks carrying our expedition stores. (Photo: Harry McAulay)*

Above   *The smiling face of a nomadic Bhutanese yak herder. (Photo: Steven Berry)*

Below   *Passing a sacred lake on Day 6 of the walk-in. (Photo: John Knowles)*

8
Gangitsawa

From the hot springs we had expected four hard days of walking to Base Camp, provided there were no more delays, and we knew that the first day would be a killer – 4,000ft of continuous steep ascent to the Nephu La, through muddy jungle. Leaving the hot springs, we crossed the Mangde Chu river, where in 1985 the Japanese had lost one of their yaks. It had been knocked off the bridge by one of the other yaks, and they had spent two abortive days searching for it downstream. The body of the yak had eventually been found, but of the equipment and box of cash it had been carrying there had been no sign. Then for hour after hour we sweated our way up out of the jungle, slipping on the mud, thigh and calf muscles aching, and cursing the weight of our rucksacks. The pass was windy, rainy and cold, and we hurried over the defile and down the other side as the rain then turned to sleet and the mist descended. On small hillocks rising a little above the otherwise marshy floor of the valley there were two yak herders' huts, thin smoke seeping out of their roofs. Jeremy Knight-Adams and I hurried towards the first of them.

Inside was a woman and her young boy. She shyly beckoned us in. Sleet poured in through the open doorway, forming a pile of snow just inside the hut. Through various holes in the roof more wet snow filtered in, and wind gusted through the rough stone wall; obviously mortar is unheard of, and I imagine mud would just get washed out by the rain. The floor had a scattering of rough planks and stones, and there was the usual yak meat and dried yak cheese hanging, blackened, from the crossbeams. Billows of blue smoke rose from a fire. The woman was barefoot, dressed in coarse yak-hair clothing, dyed black, with a single string of turquoise and jade round her neck. I saw that besides her gemstones she wore a dirty, coloured strand of cotton. She sat cross-legged next to the fire, blowing at the embers through a bamboo pipe. Her son, five or six years old, cowered behind his mother and stared open-mouthed at us in obvious fear. We sat down and shared the job of fuelling the fire while she carried on her work of kneading yak butter in a wooden tub, occasionally nodding and smiling to us.

What a hard life! No comforts of any kind, and yet she seemed content enough. We felt like intruders, and debated whether it would be all right to use a flash. We were both anxious to do nothing that would cause offence. We wanted to show her our friendship. I offered her the headphones of my Sony Walkman and she listened to some Rolling Stones, an incredulous expression on her face. Her husband and two friends arrived, knocking the snow off their clothing. The wooden handles of their long knives protruded from the folds of their *khos*. They greeted us with open delight and we were soon laughing together as they experienced rock and roll for the first time. Butter tea was offered, cup after cup – a soupy, salty liquid, its rancid taste as hard to accept as the thought of living in such a harsh environment. I ate some bread, the like of which I'd never tasted before – it was light green inside. I've no idea what it was made from, something to do with yaks I dare say.

The men wore cane hats held on by a loop of string round the back of the heads. Their skin was dark brown and their features were tougher, their eyes narrower, than the Bhutanese of the valleys. Their hands and the soles of the woman's feet were calloused, and as usual their mouths were stained red from chewing betel nut. The men wore wellington boots. They knew no other life – even travelling to Thimphu would probably be a frightening experience – and yet there we were, rich beyond their wildest imaginings, and treated like family. I loved their company, even though I couldn't understand a word spoken. A far cry from the West, where I hardly know the people on the other side of the street.

They came over to the tents in the evening to listen to Jeff on his mandolin. A girl sang us songs and played Bhutanese tunes on a bamboo whistle – the same lonely, plaintive call we had heard in Jakar.

The next day's march was a pleasure. The clouds had lifted to reveal that we were in a beautiful cirque of rocky peaks sprinkled with snow. At the end of the valley was the first of many passes leading through wild mountainous country before dropping into the region of Lunana, closed from the rest of Bhutan in the winter by snowfall. I daydreamed of just wandering through such country with a horse to carry provisions, stopping with people like those we'd met the previous night.

Our pass, the Warthang La, led us back over a ridge to the east, to above a huge gorge, at the bottom of which was the Mangde Chu river, still two or three thousand feet below us. The river has as its source the glacier at the foot of Gangkar Punsum, and from where we were standing we could just make out the snout of the Mangde Chu glacier, probably still twenty miles away in a straight line. From a little way beyond the Warthang La we should have been able to see our mountain for the first time, but the cloud was too thickly massed around the snow peaks which now formed a massive unbroken barrier on the horizon. A single lammergeier soared ahead of us amongst the crags and buttresses before being swallowed by the cloud. Although the cloud filled all the side valleys and cloaked the hillsides and mountain tops, the gigantic gorge was relatively free. We could see clearly the next two and a half days' trek, mostly contouring round mountainsides on a narrow path above the gorge, and dropping back to the Mangde Chu river on the second day. The last day would involve crossing a number of ridges of ancient glacial moraine, culminating in the highest pass of the nine days at a height of 17,000ft.

A problem arose, though. For some reason, fourteen of our forty-five yaks had failed to come up from Dur Sachu, and they were carrying much of the food. Breakfast had been a frugal affair of porridge and canned asparagus, and now we were faced with either consuming mountain rations and carrying on or waiting a day for the yaks to catch us up, if indeed they were in fact on the way. We had no way of knowing. We decided to wait a day while Yeshey and the trekking staff manager, Gopa, went back to find out what was happening.

The rest did us good, curing the usual altitude headaches, and it was timely because that day it rained continuously. The yaks arrived late that day, the ringing of the bells around their necks and the shouts and whistles of their handlers heralding their arrival through an afternoon snow shower. The following day saw us moving again.

A yak camp that the herders with us called Gangitsawa was reached at nightfall. The three yak huts appeared through the sleet that drove into our faces. It was not the French Riviera; one could not avoid stepping in either mud or yak shit, and it was well below freezing. The huts were empty and so we lit a fire in the main hut and a big group of us huddled round it trying to get warm. The place was a sordid mess – damp, cold, and miserable. I felt sorry for our trekkers, who had paid a lot of money to come with us, guilty almost that the weather was so awful, but they assured me that they couldn't care less. I think perhaps we took some pleasure from knowing that we could tolerate even the toughest conditions. The mess tent was erected in foul conditions; inside, muddy puddles covered the floor. Peter MacPherson, the cameraman, who was feeling sick, and had no will to put up his tent in the freezing, sleeting conditions, stretched out his sleeping bag in one corner and slept, oblivious of the water swilling under his foam mat.

Although we had enjoyed extraordinary hospitality from the yak handlers at Warthang, obviously the hill people are a much rougher, tougher race than people from the lower valleys, and I imagine that in such small enclosed communities friendships and enmities are strongly felt and well defined over the years. The following morning an argument started between two of the yak men. They were disputing something concerning the loads, shouting at each other full-bore. Within seconds all of them gathered round and it looked as though a fight was going to start. The loudest of the two pulled a machete-type knife out of his *kho* and brandished it above his head, straining to get at the other one, whilst Yeshey and some of our other guides tried to defuse the situation. It was an ugly moment in this most dismal spot.

A large black raven had settled on a nearby rock and made loud croaking noises at us. I found myself thinking that if there were places that were inhabited by evil spirits then Gangitsawa surely had to be one of them.

How quickly things can change! We started out in mist and drizzle cursing the weather, but before midday blue sky started to appear and soon a lot of people were stripped to the waist, soaking up the sunshine. There was now no path of any sort to follow. Yeshey showed us the way from memory. We had climbed over a number of ridges and the further we went the more beautiful the flowers and mosses became. Whole hillsides were covered with deep-blue gentians and all sorts of hard, colourful mosses, like corals. At lunch much of the cloud cleared away and at last we were confronted by an array of snowy peaks. To the north was the main Himalayan chain, a string of unnamed and unclimbed peaks separating Bhutan from Tibet. To the west were some desolate stony passes and smaller snow peaks, behind which we knew was the Lunana region. And just to the east, and below us, was the Mangde Chu glacier, massive, rubble-strewn, chaotic. Unfortunately, Gangkar Punsum was still hiding behind skirts of cloud, only the feet of her upper ridges showing. We shouted at her, willing the mists to part.

It was a leisurely day. We knew that Base Camp was only five or six hours away and for a change there was a general atmosphere of being out for a walk in the park. We dawdled along, stopping frequently for rests. Just before lunch I sat down for a rest behind Lydia and tipped her hat off with my brolly. We fought on the grass and Ginette joined in. I didn't stand a chance! Such frantic exercise left us gasping in the thin air of 16,500ft. The height was affecting us all, and upward progress was painfully slow. The last pass was the wide, rounded crest of a ridge, nothing but bare stones worn flat by the wind. A solitary prayer flag stood sending its tantric messages southwards. We sat there for a long time, soaking up the view and waiting for the cloud to clear. Gangkar Punsum must have known the significance of this moment for us, because as we sat there the clouds peeled away to reveal a perfect view of the south ridge. Everyone was spellbound. It was as though the five-million-year-old virgin was flirting with us.

The highest mountain in Bhutan could so easily have been just another big, beautiful, snowy peak. I think it is appropriate that in this mysterious country which has kept all intruders out over the centuries, and is itself such a special place, the highest mountain should be no less special. There is no easy way to the top of 'The White Peak of the Three Spiritual Brothers'. The razor-edged south ridge runs in a straight line to a perfect pyramidal summit. As if the lower difficulties were not enough, nature has placed two more final defences near the summit in the form of near-vertical rock buttresses, each several hundred feet high. On all the other faces sheer rock walls or hanging glaciers bar the way. The mountain stands in isolation, higher by far than any of its visible neighbours, though we knew that somewhere behind Gangkar Punsum was another of the world's highest unclimbed giants, Kula

Kangri, shown on some maps as being on the border but actually standing completely inside Tibet. Nobody knows what Gangkar Punsum's northern face looks like, and there seems at present to be no way of getting there.

From where we were on the pass we looked straight down on Base Camp, 500 feet below us, a rough meadow with stunted heather next to an emerald-green lake. It looked idyllic but what struck us was how far from the mountain it was. A discussion started on whether we could move our base of operations across to the other side of the glacier. Yeshey was non-committal, a sure sign that he was not happy with the idea, and in this case he was right; after our first day out on the glacier we also concluded that there was nowhere else practicable.

Yeshey is a highly intelligent and personable man, and like all Bhutanese hates to cause any kind of offence. If he wasn't happy with a particular idea he showed it by his silence, and by the subtle way he cast his eyes to the ground. We all liked him enormously, and were looking forward to climbing with him, though some problems occurred within the first few days at Base and he may have got the impression that we were unhappy with how he handled them. This was far from the truth. I do not think the problems were of his making, and I for one appreciated the efforts he made to sort them out satisfactorily.

We had at last arrived at Base Camp. The weather which we had worried so much about looked as though it was clearing, and we were especially thankful that the Japanese had not come, because it certainly would not have been feasible to have two teams on the south ridge at the same time. It was time to work again, back to the politics of trying to keep everyone happy, and the frantic rush of doing scores of jobs at the same time, in the right order, for the right reasons.

We followed the yaks down to the lake, a sacred place, according to the yak handlers, where bad luck would come to anyone throwing a stone on to the surface. In a mood of high spirits, and to prove such superstitious beliefs were not to be taken seriously, Steve Monks cast a pebble into the centre.

9

Singing the Blues

As we arrived in camp our Bhutanese staff were putting up the tents and constructing a tarpaulin kitchen in the lee of a rock. The forty-five yaks were being unloaded, and two and a half tons of equipment, film gear, and provisions lay in scattered mounds. In the confusion a couple of the yaks ran bucking and snorting through part of the camp, chased by their shouting handlers. Tobgay, the radio operator, was setting up his radio tent. The radio and petrol generator had been left there after the Austrian expedition had departed, and we wondered whether it would still work. It was a powerful set, capable of reaching Thimphu provided the weather was not too stormy, and after a day's tinkering Tobgay proudly announced that he had reported our arrival to the authorities in the capital.

Everyone was highly excited at arriving at our destination, and we gathered in knots to gaze with awe at the sheer size of Gangkar Punsum. Peter MacPherson set up the film crew's large 600mm telephoto lens, and like school kids we jostled for a close-up view of the climbing route. Gangkar Punsum, its sharp-pointed summit 8,000ft above us, was now totally free of cloud. It felt unreal to be looking at the actual detail, after poring over poor-quality prints for two years. The combination of our first clear weather and being in full sight of the peak, so enormous and difficult, brought with it a rush of adrenalin. I knew that for me fear would come later, when I was actually on the mountain, but just then I stood with the others discussing matter-of-factly the technical climbing difficulties.

During the nine-day march a feeling had grown that the bad weather was set to stay, that perhaps this year there would be no clear post-monsoon weather 'window', but now everyone began to believe that we had not got our timing wrong after all. Base Camp was bathed in hot sunshine, hardly a breath of wind stirred the air. Would it stay like this? Our Bhutanese friends were in no doubt that it would. They told us that 26 September was the day on which the country had a festival to celebrate the end of the rains, and today was 24 September. This newly learnt fact gave us cause to be hopeful, though, knowing the unpredictability of Himalayan weather, we did not place a deal of reliance on it.

After afternoon tea in the mess tent our concern at the distance of Base Camp from the mountain opened a tense discussion about our food and fuel. Since Base Camp was clearly too far to drop back to during the climbing, we would have to live at Advance Base Camp. This meant we would not be able to use the food and fuel the Bhutanese had brought for Base Camp, something we had counted on in England when calculating our mountain supplies. I could see Peter MacPherson in particular was not impressed by the possible shortage of mountain food and cooking gas. He asked why we had assumed that we would live some of the time at Base Camp. The truth was that the Japanese report had given us the idea that Base Camp was closer to the climb, and we had accordingly assumed that the film crew would live there. Now it was clear that they would have to come with us to Advance Base Camp, making matters worse. None of us had encountered a situation in which it was not possible to make good use of the Base Camp.

Steve Findlay, our food officer, was not too worried about the quantities of food, and we could always supplement our stocks by precooking rice and potatoes and taking them to Advance Base Camp, but high-altitude cooking gas was a serious problem. We had brought eighty-four cans of Epigas – enough probably for eight climbers for a month but not enough for the film crew as well.

Unfortunately, the Bhutanese kitchen staff were cooking on wood; they had practically run out of it and were pulling up stunted heathers around camp – the kind of damage to the environment none of us was happy about. There were therefore no primuses we could borrow. As a last-minute thought, we had brought my cantankerous old petrol stove – which later occupied idle hands for hours in attempts to discover why it would work for some people and not for others – but it was no solution. Al suggested we radio for a couple of stoves to be sent up with the next mail-runner. There was nothing else we could do.

The meeting broke up and Steve Monks and I went in search of Yeshey and Singey to discuss whether it was possible to trek back out a different way, via the Lunana region. Colonel Ongdi had mentioned it as a possibility in correspondence from his office in Kathmandu, but in Thimphu I had been advised to leave the decision until arrival at Base Camp. I began to understand why. There were too many uncertainties. Most important, there were a number of exposed passes, over 16,000ft, which, we were now told, often snowed up at the end of October. It would be a mistake to order the yaks from Lunana not knowing for sure whether the weather would hold good, and the yaks had to be requested via Thimphu, a minimum of twenty days in advance. It was a catch-22 situation. We had to organise the yaks but we couldn't do it until we knew what the weather would do.

At the time Steve and I wondered whether our Bhutanese friends weren't politely discouraging the Lunana idea because it would make a mess of their arrangements with the Bumthang yak people. However, we decided to abandon Lunana and trust to their local knowledge of the passes; maybe there was some reason why bad weather arrived in Lunana before it did here, we thought. There was also the fact that it was at least four days longer than the way we had come, and after a month's climbing would we really want to do a longer, even more strenuous trek out?

Inevitably on a large trip not every issue can be debated by the whole group; nothing would ever get done, and meetings can't be called every five minutes, so with some things I had fallen into a habit of taking a second opinion from Steve Monks. Monksie and I had been on two previous Himalayan trips together and over the years I had come to trust his balanced judgement. As we came out of the tent with Yeshey and Singey I noticed Harry McAulay glancing our way. I hoped Harry was not feeling cut out of the decision-making process.

People have to know everything that is going on or misunderstandings brew up unnoticed. More than anything I did not want the kind of destructive backbiting that prevents people working together. I could see no danger of this so far; I had not heard one bad thing said about anybody. We also had the advantage that all of us, apart from Ginette, had been on the last expedition to Nepal together and, as we were virtually all part of the Bristol climbing scene, we had known each other for years.

Although it was a minor blow not to be able to see Lunana, Yeshey compensated with the news that some of his Bhutanese staff and most of the yak herders were prepared to carry loads across the glacier. This was a big bonus, saving our team days of extra work, especially as under our agreement with BTC none of the Bhutanese were obliged to go any further than Base Camp. Unfortunately, however, in 1985 the Japanese had set a precedent by paying their porters for this task double the going rate of pay in Nepal. In addition, many of our trekkers had energy and ambition left to try to get to Advance Base Camp, and genuinely wanted to carry a few loads across the glacier. Collectively they had decided to stay at Base Camp two more days, even though it was now certain that they would overrun their planned 22-day itinerary.

Out of the chaos of arrival, plans were beginning to emerge. A large group of people wanted to explore the long route across the glacier to Advance Base Camp next morning, and set up our first tents there. Yeshey would go with them to help find a way through the complex moraine. I retired to my sleeping bag with a splitting headache, leaving other people to argue about what was most important to be carried across first.

Morning came and with it a perfect day. A hard frost quickly evaporated as the sun crept across the valley floor and the camp came to life. Everyone was hurrying about their own jobs; loads needed to be packed, porters instructed and lunch packs prepared. Minor disagreement is bound to take place in a large complicated task, and climbers hate being organised. Behind the gaiety generated by the excitement of the climb, minor tensions began to show. I irritably ignored advice on how to cut up the rolls of thin foam tent flooring, although whoever gave it was probably right, and Monksie just could not be bothered with the task of taking promotional shots for sponsors. He ignored the mild protests from Steve Findlay, Jeff and myself, and with a dismissive wave of the hand and a wide grin went back to packing equipment.

Though it is true that we knew largely what to expect of each other, subtle changes had taken place since our last expedition together in 1984 to Nepal. For all of us there had been large events in the intervening time, changing our lives, and perhaps, unknown to us, changing our attitudes too. I wondered how we would all get on together under stress this time. Ginette was a newcomer to our established group, replacing Dr Norman Waterhouse at the last minute, and was an attractive 28-year-old with cropped hair, similar in style to the Bhutanese monks. So far she had fitted in with us all perfectly. Her libertarian views and relaxed attitude to life in general combined with a tactful, clear-minded approach to problems had won respect from us all. Harry and Steve Findlay were occasionally prone to aggressive arguments, and some of us had worried that the fact that Monksie and Lydia had been involved with each other until recently might cause problems. However, their long relationship and 'enlightened' attitudes allowed their friendship to continue without emotional problems or rancour. The others were also worried that I would be intolerant towards Lydia because, as an organiser under stress, I had been angry that I had received only three letters from her in two years.

It is a sure fact that one of the main dangers on Himalayan expeditions is the possibility of violent rows breaking out. Climbers are strong-minded, independent people, used to doing things in their own way, and the danger is that such strong-minded individuals will not compromise, or back down, when confronted with someone else who opposes their own way of thinking. However, just as division is a main danger, so friendship is one of the most important, if not the most important, elements in an expedition.

My headache came back after lunch and I slept. Towards the end of the afternoon the others returned from a gruelling day on the glacier. They had not reached Advance Base Camp and, as we had thought, the distance to Advance Base was a full day's march. Lack of acclimatisation and unfamiliarity with the confusing route through the glacier had forced them to dump their loads under an enormous, unmistakably prominent rock just over halfway, which we labelled the 'lunch spot'. Unfortunately, the porters had forged ahead and had left their loads further up the moraine, not specifically at the site for Advance Base Camp, and there was now a worry that their boxes would be hard to find again.

The glacier crossing was not the sort where one walks across a vast expanse of flat ice, prodding the snow ahead for crevasses; it was the worst kind, a hazardous journey through a chaotic jumble of ice ridges and hillocks completely covered by rubble – anything from fist-sized rocks to boulders the size of trucks. With a heavy load to carry, the potential for slipping and breaking bones was very high.

Nevertheless I felt happy. At least the route to Advance Base Camp was roughly marked with a chain of small cairns, put there by the Japanese. All the loads had been sorted, and already a considerable amount of material was more than halfway across. The weather continued to hold and everyone was fit and healthy. I was keenly looking forward to tomorrow, to a day on the glacier myself.

Again a perfect dawn and excited activity, and while the others kitted up I rehearsed my lines for a BBC TV news interview. This time the film would be taken back with the trekkers, but thereafter we would be using a complicated system of mail-runners and couriers to deliver to London. The BBC Radio tapes, recorded daily by Harry McAulay, would follow the same route. The expedition had been financed in the main through the media, but we knew we were a side-show. If we met the King of Bhutan or, to be cynical, if someone died, or particularly if we got to the top, *then* we would probably hit national headlines, but we didn't feel the pressure of being in the full glare of the public eye. None of us suffered from being a household name.

Standing in front of the camera, I tried just to be my normal self. Film jargon, the clapper-board and the thought that this might be shown on the nine o'clock news did not help. I deliberately wore my floppy cricket hat; I did not want to be seen in the role of the formal leader. Alan said I was sounding too casual: 'You're not in the pub now, youth, give it to us again but let's have some zap in it.'

Eventually I set off an hour behind everyone else, hoping I could catch up. Rising 400 feet behind the camp there was a ridge, again covered in gentians and red, yellow and pale green mosses, and from its crest I looked down on the glacier, twisting past the southern toe of the mountain. Its main bulk swung down from the peaks to the north, a string of sharp snow- and ice-plastered mountains forming a chain on the very border between Bhutan and Tibet. I could see the site for Advance Base Camp at the head of a snow bowl, itself feeding a small glacier merging with the main river of ice that I had to cross. The site was unthreatened by any possibility of avalanche and conveniently sat virtually at the very foot of the south ridge.

I started the descent into the bowels of the glacier, following one cairn after another. The mountains were lost from view, the sun beat down and the only sound was the occasional crash of boulders tumbling down nearby slopes. I caught up with Harry McAulay, Peter Santamera, John Knowles and the three porters at the

'Ovaltine rock', a distinctive boulder perched on a mushroom of ice with a Japanese can of Ovaltine next to it. It marked the end of the main crossing. Monksie, who like me had not been across before, had shot ahead of everyone else, and Harry had seen him picking a different line through the centre of the glacier. As the day wore on and we still saw no sign of him we worried that he might be lying somewhere with a broken leg, or worse. We had not counted on his speed. He was hours ahead of us.

I had a lunch of cold boiled potatoes and hot chilli dip with Harry, who confessed to me that this would be his last big expedition. He was still having trouble with his chest, something that plagued him on the Nepalese expedition. Harry was a former Royal Marine Officer, his chiselled good looks and moustache a perfect caricature for that breed of the toughest of fighting men. One of the largest and strongest men I know, I was used to him regularly throwing me around like a bale of straw, but at high altitude his strength did him no good. He just did not acclimatise well. He was also thinking of his girl-friend, Antoinette, and I think he felt it was unfair on her that he was taking such large risks. At any rate, by the end of the climb he had concluded that adventurer he was, but Himalayan climber he was not.

It looked like an easy hour from the 'lunch spot', but we were badly mistaken. We had added to our loads from yesterday's dump and our pace slowed to a crawl. The shifting maze of huge granite blocks forming the moraine on the northern side of the snow bowl was even more difficult to negotiate than the lower half of the glacier.

Steve Monks breezed past on his way down again. 'Not long now, lads. Half an hour, probably. You can't miss it. I've put a tent up. It's right where the Japs had their camp – I even found some packets of soy sauce. They've built half a dozen level platforms amongst the rocks next to the glacier. Just stuff the loads inside. 'Fraid I haven't spotted the porters' loads from yesterday though. See you later.'

An hour went by; still no tent. Peter Santamera caught me up and passed me. The afternoon was drawing on and cloud moved into the basin. As the dome tent appeared, so it started to snow. The trip to Advance Base Camp was a long way in one direction, and now we had to go all the way back again. I felt completely drained. What a relief it was to drop the supplies out of my sack!

By this time the porters had got scared by the snowstorm and had turned back, so that there were now more lost loads sitting on one of an infinite number of similar-looking rocks.

I stumbled slowly along, head lolling, trying to keep something in reserve, trying to maintain sufficient concentration to avoid twisting an ankle. My brolly kept off the worst of the snow but my hands froze holding it. Harry hung back, giving me encouragement, though I only had energy to answer him in monosyllables. In earlier years I would have felt like crying in despair by this stage, but now perhaps I had learnt the meditative art of ignoring pain.

The light was fading as we came over the final ridge, nine or ten hours after leaving. Phuntso was waiting with a cup of tea, but all I wanted was to lie down and sleep. I felt so desperately tired that I could not imagine being able to get up again for our trekkers' 'last supper'. I knew I had to be there, and hoped that perhaps they would just prop me up in one corner, present in body if nothing else.

There was a sad, expectant atmosphere in the mess tent an hour later, and supper was eaten in comparative silence. I was still trying to surface from my tiredness, trying to make the brain work, to sort out the right things to say. These men had become our best friends. We had shared a time together that was far beyond everyday life. We had witnessed an ancient culture virtually cut off from the outside world, shared hardships, enjoyed a rare and special comradeship, and now they had to leave, just as we started to risk our lives on a climb that was obviously going to be extremely serious.

The whole evening was to turn into one of the most emotional times I've ever experienced with other people. Complete silence followed the serving of coffee and, although I knew I was expected to make a speech, the power to utter sufficient thanks still eluded me. John Knowles, the exuberant elder statesman of our new friends, finally stirred me out of my lethargy with an utterly sincere speech of his own. He thanked us for the best time he had ever had, saying also that he knew we would get to the top with the spirit we had between us. I recall now the great sadness we all felt knowing that the unique time we had shared was coming to an end. After my own reply the formality disappeared and everybody each confessed his or her feelings, whilst the last bottles of Glenfiddich and Maker's Mark whisky were passed round. Maggie came over and kissed me, to raucous cheering. For the two of us it was the end of two years of immensely hard work, strain, argument, and finally success in putting the support trek together. We had had our differences along the way, and the money side of things was still not over, but at that moment it was all forgotten; we were as close as we would ever get.

The tent was packed. The Bhutanese were there, yak men as well, and before too long we were a swaying, laughing bunch of pissed people singing song after song, *ad infinitum*, or contributing with anything we could think of. John Knowles recited 'Lucy Grace' by William Wordsworth, and I was astonished how many half-forgotten poems could be dredged from people's memories. The yak men, shy and embarrassed, but with encouragement, sang two of our favourite lilting Bhutanese love songs, and Lydia performed a brave and emotional solo of a tearful Joan Baez classic. Allen Jewhurst slipped back into the slang and jargon of his native East End of London, treating us to a number of crafty Cockney melodies, people roaring with laughter at the bawdy lyrics. We sang until our voices were hoarse, gargled with whisky, and sang again.

The tent was lit by one candle and a couple of dim battery-powered fluorescent tubes. Snow fell on the roof, and occasionally someone would get up and knock it all off. People lay in heaps for warmth. I noticed Steve Findlay dozing and waking, and also that he had run out of cigarette papers and was rolling his tobacco in air-mail paper. The mandarin eyes of Harry Jensen blinked like an owl in one corner. Jeff Jackson jammed with his mouth-organ in another. Flash-bulbs went off, and as we bellowed one of the loudest choruses, each of us trying to outdo the other, Lydia struggled through the morass of bodies to hug everyone. We progressed through whole eras of pop – Beatles songs, the Stones, Dylan, Cliff Richard, Lonnie Donegan – and when we ran low we turned to nursery rhymes, carols, bawdy rugby songs, Auld Lang Syne and the national anthem. The energy stayed with us for five solid hours. Just when we thought it was finished some new theme would occur to us and the volume built back again. We quite literally could not stop, and no one would have dreamt of leaving. By midnight many of us had fallen asleep leaning against one another.

We were still singing as we finally left the mess tent in the early hours, stumbling through the newly fallen snow to our sleeping bags, the happiest stage of our adventure all but over.

Above   *Sunset at 21,000ft, Chomolhari on the right-hand horizon. (Photo: Steve Findlay)*

Left   *Gangkar Punsum from Base Camp. (Photo: Harry McAulay)*

Overleaf   *Camp 1 and views of unexplored country to the south-west. (Photo: Steven Berry)*

10
Shortages

The next morning four or five inches of snow covered the ground and it was still falling lightly. Naturally, our friends wanted to be off early in case it became worse, and we knew that, as it was, it would be a laborious struggle for them crossing the 17,000ft pass behind Base Camp, where the new snow could be up to their knees.

Those of us remaining frantically tried to hold them back as we finished scribbling last-minute letters to families and friends and telexes for media and sponsors. Finally the trekkers tore themselves away, and we watched and shouted to them as they pulled up the hillside and into the dense cloud covering the top of the pass.

The camp seemed quiet and empty without them. We had become so used to them being with us day after day that it was a shock to be on our own. It was a worse wrench for them. We had experienced such an intense time together, and now they had to leave us, knowing the fatal reputation that Himalayan climbing has, and now with full comprehension of the size and steepness of one of the highest unclimbed peaks in the world.

From John Knowles's diary – 27 September

'Today was probably the most emotional day of my life. Is that an exaggeration? Don't think so. I've been married, had two kids been divorced, lost both parents, etc., etc., but I can never remember feeling as cut up as I do this afternoon. Am writing this in a very cold and draughty yak herder's hut, four hours back on the way home from Base Camp, trying to keep composure in front of the others – with great difficulty. I'm not ashamed to say that today I shed more tears than at any time since my childhood. I left Base Camp first because after saying goodbyes I wanted to be on my own. Went round saying emotional goodbyes to all the climbers, especially those three great guys Jackson, Finders and Monks, and then Steve Berry, who, although this being my first expedition I had nothing to compare it against, had been in my book a good leader, usually cheerful, always helpful and approachable, and who treated us trekkers as one of the team, who were all equal. The hardest goodbye was to Lydia – that amazing Kiwi, who made more of an impression on me in those 2½ weeks than any woman before. I gave her my Wainwright neckerchief and told her to plant it on the top – if anyone will, she will.

'I set off with a huge lump in my throat, crossed the river, and started up the steep climb on the other side, when across the valley came the sound of Steve Berry calling "Bye, John." This completely creased me, and I just sat down on a rock and unashamedly burst into tears. We'd had such a fantastic and amazing time with these 22 people – *all* of whom I'd go with again, and I knew we'd never be all together again, and I felt so proud that I'd been part of it, yet so cut up that it was all over. These last four hours are something I wouldn't want again, and yet I suppose to have such an experience on the expedition, it's worth having to endure it.

'Hope the next few days won't be an anticlimax – it seems so empty without the climbers – my thoughts keep going back to the mountain and wondering how they are getting on. Wish I was with them. Must pull myself together – get the Travel Scrabble out, do the duvet jacket up tighter. Oh gawd – not rice and chillies again tonight!'

Now that they had gone it was just us and the mountain. Only the climbing occupied our thoughts.

Back home we had often talked over the style of the ascent we wanted to adopt. Ideally, we wanted to climb to the summit in one continuous push from Advance Base, or, if the technical difficulties were too great to be quickly overcome, to establish two or three camps whilst we worked on the difficult sections. We wanted to keep a completely open mind on how things would be done because, firstly, we had expected to be allotted the west face, about which there was practically no information, and, second, nobody had actually climbed the mountain by any route. All we had to work from was a copy of the 1985 Japanese report, with its photographs of the south ridge and Japanese text.

We were also a team of varying abilities, and had talked about the possibility of splitting the group into two teams – one to go purely Alpine-style, the other to climb to within two or three days of the summit by establishing a number of camps. The first team could acclimatise by helping the others establish their route. Our final decision on the method would depend entirely on the difficulty of the route and the fitness and inclination of all of us at the time.

At that time back in England I had corresponded with the Japanese leader, who told me he had permission for the south ridge. Our own permit was not specific when it came to which route we were to have; after all, the authorities would have no more idea of what was possible on the mountain than anyone else. But if the Japs were going to be given their original route, the south ridge, then we expected that we would have to somehow find a way up the west face. Now, with the Japanese having dropped out of the picture, we had eyes only for the plum line, the south ridge. It was clear that this would not 'go' Alpine-style; the rock sections were too steep. We therefore planned to put in two camps and live at the top one until we had 'fixed' the rock steps, and then a group of us would take off for the summit in a three- or four-day push.

Here was a moment of test, our first meeting to discuss the initial tactics of the climb to Camp 1. How would people see their own personal game now that we had arrived and could see what it was all about? Would there be difficulties in jockeying for position, or would the decisions flow easily from the happy team spirit we had so far enjoyed? We all quickly agreed that four people should move across and live at Advance Base Camp, and start climbing to Camp 1, whilst the rest ferried the remaining loads across the glacier. But who wanted to establish Camp 1? Ginette was not too keen as she had no experience of the job of fixing ropes in snow and ice.

Monksie and Jeff on past performance were our strongest pair. Jeff had been to 26,000ft on Cho Oyu in Nepal and had still felt strong at that height, and Monksie had been above 23,000ft two or three times, though it was true he sometimes had trouble acclimatising. He was undoubtedly our most experienced ice climber, with a recent solo ascent of the North Face of the Eiger to his credit. Already he had shown that at these lower altitudes he was moving faster than anyone else. I hoped that they would both be happy to hang back at this stage.

On the other hand Lydia had also been to 23,000ft and was a strong, bold lead climber. Would there be other resentment if she pushed herself forward too much? After all, she had done no work at all towards the organisation or raising money for the expedition, as she had been living in New Zealand for the last two years. Back in Thimphu she had made a point of expressing her worry about this to me. Now she sat and listened as other people made open their own ambitions. I was relieved that she was waiting and watching, and not pushing her own desires too early.

Without it being said, we all knew where Harry stood. He had no pretensions to a lead climbing role, and like Ginette he lacked experience in placing 'dead men' (snow anchors) for securing the fixing ropes. If the route went well and he was fit he would try to climb as high as possible, maybe even to the summit, but his attitude was that he would do whatever was best for the team effort. He had been badly disappointed on the last expedition to Cho Oyu, where his chest trouble had kept him mainly at Base Camp. Not willing to admit that he can be beaten by anything, for the sake of his own pride he wanted to prove that he could climb high.

I had thought about my own position for some time. The fact is that I am not a brilliant technical climber. I had examined the route closely and knew that the top rock sections would be beyond my ability to lead. I therefore wanted to be involved in the route finding in the lower half of the mountain and said this to the others. They agreed that it sounded sensible.

Steve Findlay wanted to get out into the lead, which suited me. I was expecting this as I thought he would want to find out how the altitude was going to affect him. Like Harry, he had had his problems on our expedition to Cho Oyu, where he had had stomach trouble so severe that he had spent a week in hospital after his return to England. Camp 2, at a height of 21,000ft, had been his limit, and he had stayed there a few days feeling weak and debilitated. Had it really been his stomach or was it the altitude that had prevented him from reaching the highest camps?

The foursome would be made up by Lydia and Yeshey. When we arrived in Bhutan, Yeshey had taken us to his house in Thimphu, a comfortable log cabin on the outskirts. In his living room mountain pictures hung on the walls and his crampons, axe, and helmet were propped in one corner. Here was a devoted climber. He had already climbed several smaller peaks in Bhutan, and was one of a handful of tourist guides chosen to receive training at a mountain centre in Japan. More than anything, it was his fervent ambition to be the first Bhutanese to climb the highest mountain in their kingdom.

The next morning we all set off for Advance Base Camp, but at the start of the glacier we unanimously decided that the crossing looked too dangerous. With four or five inches of snow covering the rubble the chances of breaking a leg seemed too high. A day's sunshine would get rid of it. Nevertheless, I felt guilty at wasting such a beautiful sunny day. While the others drifted back to camp, Al Jewhurst and I decided we would walk up an easy ridge nearby to a small rocky outcrop.

Two and a half hours of easy snow plodding brought us to the top, from where we could see that we were higher than Advance Base Camp. From our rocky eyrie we had a better view of the barren, desolate terrain leading westwards to Lunana. It was country begging to be explored – uninhabited, trackless, a region of small glaciers, 20,000ft peaks, rocky spires, and passes guarding secrets I would have loved to investigate. We lounged in the sun for a while, and I remember Al saying, 'These are the days you dream about back in England, Steve. Enjoy it while it lasts because this is it, kid, this is what it's all about.'

When we got back to camp it was a very different story. A group of disgruntled people sat outside their tents complaining that no lunch had been served, and no brew of tea had been ready when they returned from the glacier. Over the previous few days we had noticed that a number of foodstuffs had either run out or were obviously in short supply. Now there were no biscuits. A serious crisis indeed! Harry in particular voiced the general feeling that the kitchen staff were lazy, that breakfast was getting later each day, and that requests were being ignored.

Al and I went to the mess tent to find out from Yeshey and Gopa what the problem was. Al, in an uncharacteristic, undiplomatic way, waded in, saying that his film company had paid a lot of money to Bhutan and he expected to receive better service, and that if the kitchen staff could not perform then they should be changed. I hurriedly tried to calm the situation, saying that I was sure that it was just a question of them understanding more fully what we expected of them. During the trek we had not got to know them, as we had been so involved with the trekkers, but now it was important that they were our friends. Yeshey apologised and assured us that Phuntso, Dorji and Kencho (the kitchen staff) were just as anxious to please us, but that they became confused when requests came from several different people at once.

The food problem was a different matter. Yeshey admitted that there were shortages. Ginette, in the mess tent reading, said, 'Yeshey, do you know just exactly what food you do have? I mean, have you any idea how many days it will all last? Have you got a list of what's left so that we can work it out?'

Yeshey then surprised us by saying that he had thought that food was only supposed to be supplied *to* Base Camp, and not actually *at* Base Camp. This came as a shock to me, and, worrying that I'd made a serious mistake, I dug out from my file the Bhutanese Mountaineering Rules and Regulations. They stated clearly that Yeshey was under a misapprehension. Obviously acutely embarrassed, he and Gopa agreed to carry out a stock-taking immediately so that we could see what needed to be ordered by radio.

An hour later the food list was produced. It was obvious we would not starve – there were plenty of staple foods – but all the 'goodies' would run out. Within a few days we would be out of jams, tinned meat, chutney, coffee and all those things that make eating at altitude a bearable business. Yeshey was full of apology; they had never had such a large group as ours and had made some bad mistakes in their calculations.

Outside the mess tent I met Lydia and Peter MacPherson. In their anger at finding that we were short of food they both cynically suggested that it was a rip-off by the authorities. They pointed at the very high prices charged to expeditions, making Bhutan possible for only the rich or determined and putting it out of the reach of the small expeditions, and now they felt that we weren't even getting our money's worth. It was a very heated moment, with things said in anger that would be regretted later, and I knew that Yeshey and Gopa would be unhappily listening to all this from within the mess tent. Part of Lydia and Pete's distrust, I think, came from not having got to know the authorities in Thimphu. I had carried out all the dealings with the Bhutan Tourist Corporation and had found them to be completely friendly and reasonable. I could not believe there was the remotest chance that this shortage had been deliberately planned, and said so. I felt sure that it was purely a mistake born from inexperience in dealing with large expeditions. After all, we were only the twelfth into Bhutan since they opened up their mountains in 1983, and we were by far the largest. Anger is a destroyer of reason. Had we not, after all, enjoyed first-class treatment and hospitality in the capital?

The problem with ordering more food was that it would take yaks eight or nine days to come up from Bumthang, and in any case practically all of us would soon be living at Advance Base Camp and above. Certainly Chris Lister and Mark Stokes, of the film crew, would spend most of their time at Base, and there might be others there if we suffered any illnesses. It was also important that we had enough food for the walk-out. However, the situation was improved by Yeshey and Gopa having earlier clubbed together to buy one of the yaks for meat. The severed head of this unfortunate animal was placed by Phuntso on top of the kitchen rock. It was a grisly reminder of the origin of the meat we now ate at Base until the end of the trip. That was if you had the good fortune, or the bad luck – whichever way you looked at it – to be in Base Camp. We decided to request two weeks' food for six people, besides the walk-out supplies, at the prearranged radio call early the next morning.

The general bad mood and bitching continued at supper, though thankfully the happy disposition of our cook, Phuntso, was not affected by the afternoon's unpleasantness. After the usual noodle soup he ducked through the doorway, grinning widely, proudly carrying our first dish of fried yak meat, with rice, radishes, and of course more chillies than was prudent for our less hardened stomachs. Most of the others liked yak but I found the taste of the meat too strong and had difficulty overcoming an impulse to throw up. I'm not sure what was worse – eating the meat or being ribbed unmercifully by the others for my squeamishness.

It was clear that the other kitchen staff were also making a marked effort to be as helpful and attentive as possible, obviously at pains to put things right. I sincerely hoped they were harbouring no bad feelings.

Everyone was up and away early the next morning, except me. I had to stay to talk over our problem with Karchung Wangchuck at the nine o'clock radio call. Tobgay was trying to improve reception by stringing a reel of copper wire between poles up the small hillside next to his tent. The generator chugged away, charging a pair of car batteries and fouling the air with its petrol fumes. Inside the wigwam-style tent four of us squeezed round the Japanese radio set. After half an hour of listening to whistles and squeaks, with Tobgay stoically tapping continuously on the Morse key, we started to receive a reply. At first it was just Morse but with Tobgay fiddling with the controls we established a strong enough contact to switch to the microphone. At times the reception was near-perfect, but then it would deteriorate to a point where we resorted to shouting our messages repeatedly. When the garbled reply came back we would all crane forward and, at the end of Thimphu's message, look at each other, grimace, shake our heads and laugh.

Karchung gradually picked up the picture, and promised to send supplies by horse and yak as fast as possible. I thought he had understood the quantities but I was not sure.

Out in the sunshine I hefted my sack, waved a cheery goodbye and prepared for the long, agonising flog over the rubble pile to Advance Base Camp. Yesterday's sun had indeed burnt off the thin layer of snow, and with two ski-sticks to help me balance I teetered across the maze of granite blocks and through the hillocks of ice.

As a principle I only use the Sony Walkman when there is drudgery to endure and when I know I'm not missing anything. I was definitely not missing anything in this wasteland, and David Bowie and the Rolling Stones kept me reasonably happy for the six hours to camp. I felt pleased at feeling much stronger than before, and, much to the amusement of Steve Findlay, whose head poked out of a tent at hearing my calls for a cup of tea, I even ran the last twenty yards into camp.

11
The Ramp

Examining the mountain from Base Camp, we had wondered whether it would be possible to take a short cut to the site for Camp 2 by cutting across the north-western flank of the main ridge. We would then miss out the hump in the ridge that we called the 'snow dome' and save ourselves days of needless effort. However, from Advance Base Camp a sight of the north-western flank was obscured by a rocky subsidiary ridge, and so on 30 September Findlay, Lydia and I set off on a recce to obtain a view of the flank. Yeshey, meanwhile, had gone off in search of the various loads abandoned by the porters, more concerned with his duties as our liaison officer than with missing a day's climbing.

It was a misty, still day as we plodded along on the hard snow to the end of the glacial bowl. Twenty minutes from Advance Base Camp we came to an ice slope, caused by a fold in the glacier. We clipped on our crampons, unstrapped our axes and enjoyed again the feeling of kicking the front points into the ice and the sound that an axe makes as its curved point thunks into the shiny surface. After fifty feet we were at the top and again crunching along on nearly level snow. We moved in slow motion, the high altitude making us gasp heavily for air. As we approached the subsidiary ridge the slopes steepened and we slowed to thirty paces at a time. In between each effort we leant on our axes, heads resting on folded arms, until a level breathing rate had returned and we could face another thirty steps.

We crossed some old avalanche debris – only a minor slide, but enough of a reminder of the danger for us to be nervous. We kept a wary eye on the slopes above. The three of us zigzagged upwards towards three rock pinnacles at the top of the subsidiary ridge where it merged into the northern flank. The cold mist was dispelled as the sun rose higher, and to add to the exhausting labour came the heat and the glare. Past experience, and a sensitive English skin, had taught me the lesson of caking every exposed area with high-altitude cream, and of wearing a large floppy hat with a handkerchief pinned to the back to protect my neck. I remember seeing on a previous Himalayan trip the lips of a friend of mine who had not put on his lipsalve blow up like balloons to such a size that he could not eat solids for days. Later his lips split, causing him a great deal of pain.

There was a blustery wind when we arrived at the pinnacles, and a dizzy drop on the other side which dictated extreme caution near the edge. Gingerly we leant round the pinnacles. We didn't have to look twice: it was immediately obvious that there was no short cut to Camp 2. The northern flank was in reality nothing like its appearance from Base Camp.

From our new vantage-point we could see the summit again, with the plume of cloud that we had noticed was usually there, blowing southwards. The spectacle of the day, though, was undoubtedly the uninterrupted view of the gigantic west face, several miles in breadth and some five or six thousand feet high – designed by its maker to stop people like us climbing up it! In its whole length every possible line of ascent was blocked either by hanging glaciers or by mammoth granite walls. There was just one tenuous line of interconnecting ice fields that offered a slim possibility, and even that was under some threat by seracs in its lower third. At the base of the stupendous wall, a thousand feet below us, the crumpled, cracked surface of another glacier guarded the approach. I made a mental note that it would take a lot of route finding, and several days from Base, just to get to the foot of the face.

Now that the northern flank was ruled out we descended towards the snow bowl, taking a close look at the other alternatives for gaining the south ridge proper. We did not like the look of the Japanese gully, for, although it was a clear and simple route to follow, its lower half was threatened by some unstable-looking seracs, and we already knew that one of the Japanese climbers had been avalanched down it for a thousand feet. Luckily, she survived.

We traversed under the face, hoping that we might find the way the Austrians had recently taken, but there was no sign of their old fixed ropes. However, we spotted a fairly narrow ramp of snow passing diagonally between steep rock buttresses and leading to a point on the Japanese gully which was above the threat of the seracs. It looked quite feasible, but at the end of the ramp was a short section of steep rock and ice to gain the Jap gully. This section looked so short, perhaps only a hundred feet, that we thought there must be a way up it somehow. From Advance Base Camp this ramp was hidden from view, and with its discovery it now seemed that the day spent on reconnaissance had not been wasted after all.

The same could not be said for Yeshey's day. He had not been able to locate the missing loads. He looked rather dejected, but thought that Phuntso would know where they were as he had been with the yak men the day they made their mistake. In truth I felt sure that they would be found sooner or later. Al and Pete greeted us with mugs of instant coffee from our mountain supplies, and while we had been out in the midday sun they had transformed Advance Base Camp by an extensive building programme. The chaos was now organised. We had a larder, an equipment store, a kitchen, and a toilet area away from the water supply. I came in for some criticism, though, because my old petrol stove was not working properly. We had tested it before leaving, but now it spat and flared at anyone who went near it. It was waiting for its owner's touch, and to my satisfaction I soon had it purring nicely.

The next morning at 5.45 a.m. I lay with just my nose sticking out of my sleeping bag listening to the snow falling outside. I was warm, comfortable and sleepy. I was glad we didn't have to get up. My lazy self hoped that perhaps we could stay there today, reading, talking and playing cards. I could teach Lydia some more chess moves. The inside of the tent was coated with frost, and my water bottle under a pillow of spare clothes had frozen. At least if I kicked the piss bottle over it would not be a disaster, I thought idly. The head-torch batteries had suffered in the night and only a dim light illuminated the frozen zip of the door as I took a look outside. Cloud everywhere, no good. Findlay, Lydia and I lay waiting. Before going to sleep the previous night talk of going above 20,000ft up the ramp and finding Camp 1 – the first real climbing – had kept us awake for hours. Like the head-torch batteries, our full charge of enthusiasm had suffered with the night's frost.

Half an hour later there was silence – no pitter-patter of snow on the tent. The clouds were clearing.

'Hey, Berry sahib, your turn to cook breakfast. Give him a kick, Lyd. I'll have sausage, mushrooms, eggs, beans, bacon, on toast please,' said Findlay.

'Yes, and while you're at it the same for me, Steve,' added Lydia.

The night temperature of −15°C meant that I wore all my clothes inside my sleeping bag, and at least I didn't have to get dressed. In fact the same clothes stayed on all the time we were on the mountain. When I finally came to take it off the thermal underwear was covered in a white powder – dead skin which had been replaced during the month's climbing. The only physical struggle that morning was in forcing the felt inner boots into the plastic outer shells and fumbling with the laces, frozen hard like wire. Outside, the last few bright stars were winking out as another day began. The summit caught the first rays of sun and for the first fifteen minutes turned a beautiful shell-pink.

Fifty yards from the camp there was a small frozen pond where we collected our water. I picked my way across the moraine, feeling like an automaton, still deeply drugged by sleep. I smashed the four inches of ice on the pond with an axe, banging my knuckles in the process. The pain brought me fully out of sleep for a few seconds, making me swear. I filled the large cooking pot with water and stumbled to the kitchen.

The petrol stove did not seem to recognise its owner and after a protracted argument with the bloody thing I gave up and used a gas cylinder. I took round cups of warm muesli and coffee to the others, who by now were halfway packed.

By 8 a.m. we were on the move. My chest hurt from suppressed laughter at Findlay's ritualistic mumblings on the unfair nature of life as he trudged up the glacier towards the ramp. The pack was heavy on my back and now that the sun was up I was sweltering. Count twenty steps, stop, pant for breath, do another twenty. My legs could take it but my heart and lungs could never make the adjustment.

To gain the ramp we had to climb up the side of a large cone of snow, some four hundred feet high, which lay between two huge rock buttresses. Vertically above it was a large snow field which occasionally emptied minor streams of powder snow down a couple of ice gullies on to the top of the cone.

As we neared the top of the cone, where the granite buttresses squeezed in towards me, the angle steepened and my two axes started to become useful. A slip here would not be serious – there was no vertical drop over cliff edges and the snow cone would act as a safety net – but I began to feel the exposure of being high above the snow bowl. We passed the ice gullies on our left – vertical, intimidating, trickles of powder snow shushing on to the cone. Dead ahead was a small rock wall with a snow ledge at its base. A last effort up soft snow which kept giving way, meaning that every three steps up were two steps down, and we were standing on a safe spot where we could belay and rest. At the right-hand edge of the ledge and round a corner the snow slope disappeared, looking steeper than anything so far. Lydia went to take a look, unroped, and after about twenty feet came back protesting that the snow was hollow and in danger of avalanching. There was no safety net now; we had traversed sufficiently far right to take us above one of the large rock buttresses. The rope came out and Lydia tied on and tried a line closer to the rock. She disappeared from sight. We stamped our feet in the cold shadow of the rock as the rope slowly paid out. Her shout came faintly: 'OK, I've made it! I'm on the ramp and I've fixed the rope. Clip on and come on round.'

Rounding the corner the ramp looked a lot steeper than we had imagined, and as I peered up at the worst section of rock and ice at the top, still four hundred feet above us, I worried that this could all be a waste of effort. Up above Yeshey and me, Steve and Lydia were creeping up the ramp. They were less than enthusiastic, worried at the condition of the snow. The slope was now at an angle which made me wonder about the mechanics of what was keeping it all there, especially as the top layer was so sugary. I suppressed my fear by concentrating on what was in front of me, kicking hard at the slope and sinking my axes into the neat lines of holes Steve and Lydia had left. It was easy really, once you got used to it, and as the snow became harder and icier the higher we went so the axes slammed in solidly. After every twenty steps, while resting, I would snatch a glance at the two above. Findlay was in the lead now, and right at the top, where the ramp narrowed to an icy runnel. He started to edge his way between the rocks whilst Lydia waited. I stopped to watch.

He made very slow progress, splayed out between the rocks, trying to make handholds by chipping the snow and ice off the embedded boulders with his axe. The small chunks of ice and piles of spindrift whistled down. I lay against the slope, my hand over my head for protection. He climbed to the left, up the side of a large rock, his crampons sending off sparks as they scraped and slipped on the granite. My heart was in my mouth; it looked as if he might fall off, but with a desperate heave he stood on top of the rock. Morbidly I had found myself thinking of Angela, his wife, and their son Ben, and what I would have said had he fallen.

Steve shouted down: 'Lyd, look, I can't find anything to tie on to here, and I'm going to have to down-climb this, because there is no way on above, but it was bloody difficult getting up, so what I'll do is I'll throw you a rope down, and what I want you to do is climb up to that lump sticking in the ice, yeah, that one way over on the right. Tie on if you can, and I'll back down, with you giving me some protection from the rope. OK?'

'OK, Steve.'

Lydia cautiously climbed up through the rocks and more ice lumps spun down. I moved up to take her place at the top of the ramp to get out of the line of fire. Everything was happening so slowly; I wanted so much for this danger to be over and to be able to relax again. I saw her get to the lump on the right.

Her worried voice shouted, 'Steve, there's nothing I can tie on to. I'll just have to sit on top of it – it's the best there is.'

'Well, OK then, but watch it carefully. There's a chance I could come off on this.'

I turned my eyes away, and then thought, 'No, I must watch. If there's an accident people will ask me what happened.' I tilted my head back again to stare as Steve scraped and slithered his way down without mishap. So far so good. He moved over to Lydia and continued climbing above and out of sight. Time passed agonisingly slowly, and all that happened was the fairly constant stream of ice lumps and snow from above.

Then a shout: 'I'm up at the Japanese gully, and I can see their old fixed ropes. I'm safe enough here. You can come up now, Lyd.'

I felt weak at the knees with relief. More time passed, more snow and ice clattered down, and eventually there was another shout and the rope whistled down. It was a perfect shot, but the end lay a tantalising twelve feet from my grasp on the small rock wall above my head.

'Hey, Lydia, I need some more rope. I can't reach it from here. Send me down a bit more.'

'There isn't any more. You'll have to climb up to it,' she replied.

'I can't do that, it's up the rock wall. Just tie some slings on your end or something.'

Nothing happened. Obviously Lyd thought I was being a wimp for not being able to reach another ten feet, and that if she waited I would be forced to do something. I was getting angry.

'Lydia, for fuck's sake I can't reach the end. I've got to have another ten feet. Tie some slings on your end, can't you?' I shouted at the top of my voice. Climbing's good for that; nobody gives a damn if you shout at them.

After a while the rope snaked down and I tied on and started up the rotten snow above the ice runnel at the end of the ramp. Shortly I came to the big rock on the left. Steve shouted down that he had left a 500 foot coil of fixing rope on the top of it, to make it easier for him to lead the pitch, but I would have to pick it up. There are some things one just has to do, and this was one of them; there was no way I could chicken out. Halfway up the rock one crampon caught in a crack. Lungs bursting, I practically cried out in frustration and fear. I could see now exactly why Steve had nearly come off. I was fighting to keep my feet bridged out on the rock as I fumbled to feel the poor handholds above through three layers of bulky mitts. My two axes hanging from wrist loops were a hindrance. Desperation provided strength, but when it was over and I stood up on top of the rock my lungs worked painfully to redress the oxygen debt. For a good five minutes they sucked at the partial vacuum before, little by little, my body regained equilibrium. I wish I could say the same for my mental state. I was terrified.

I now stood on the tiniest of pedestals with the prospect of having to go back down the way I had just come. The chances of a fall seemed almost certain, and the rope from above disappeared off diagonally to the right, meaning that if I did fall I would go for a big swing, with the risk of the rope severing on the protruding rocks, or me careering into them. First, though, I had to take off my heavy sack and put inside the 500 feet of fixing line. I worked as carefully as I could, taking off the sack; to drop it now would be disastrous. I put it back on only to find that I had tangled the rope somehow. I whimpered and cursed myself for not being more careful and repeated the procedure.

I stood looking down the rock, trying to force myself to do it. I sought reassurance from above. 'I'm very frightened about this. Have you got a good belay?'

I should never have asked as the reply was, 'Well, it's not absolutely bomber. Try not to come off unless you can't help it.'

A small part of me giggled insanely amongst the clamour of fear, as the thought rose and was dismissed that they might be winding me up. I took a hold of myself, turned round, faced in, every part of me trembling, my eyes frantically darting from one hold to another, total panic close at hand. From somewhere a calmness appeared. A fish out of water would have looked in better shape than I did then, but I managed to slow down my movements from being a pattern of wild scrabbling to a series of deliberate, calculated actions that did get me back down again.

I was by now completely shattered; my heart was thumping quite painfully inside my ribcage and my body heaved for more air. The steep climbing was still ahead but at least I now had the rope above me. I no longer cared about the drop below; all I wanted to do was to finish the torture. Encouragement was coming from above, and I felt a glow of gratitude: they knew what I was going through, they understood. There were small sections of vertical rock and ice above, and the rest was not far off being the same angle. Bit by bit I hacked and kicked my way up, progress reduced to five or ten steps at a time. Findlay's head peered down at me, grinning. Just the last few steps, and then I was sitting astride a knife-edged arête, hugging Lydia.

The rope was dropped to Yeshey, who had said hardly a word since we started up the ramp, and he now climbed up to us with the minimum of fuss. I confess feeling a little envy at the comparative ease with which he had mastered the hard section. I am sure he had started the day feeling a little self-concious, climbing with these foreign stars, but now he had proved his ability. We were impressed.

It had started to snow and there was no chance of going further that day. We had intended that Findlay and Lydia would stay at Camp 1, but in any case I had forgotten Lyd's sleeping bag and the two of them had left their Kariamats behind. The main thing was that we had cracked the route. It only remained for us to follow the Jap line to Camp 1.

A large orange rock with a flat top make a convenient place to dump our loads, and quickly we fixed the 500-foot reel of rope to the Japanese anchors, which I noticed wryly were perfectly secure, and abseiled back down the ramp. We whooped with raw excitement as we bum-slid down the bottom of the snow cone, finally floundering across the glacier into camp, bodies spent. No matter whether it was Sunday tomorrow or not, it would be a day of rest for the four of us.

Above *Easy climbing on the ridge above Camp 1.* (*Photo: Steven Berry*)

Below *Nearing the top of the snow dome, the summit of Gangkar Punsum in the background.* (*Photo: Steven Berry*)

Overleaf *Camp 2.* (*Photo: Steven Berry*)

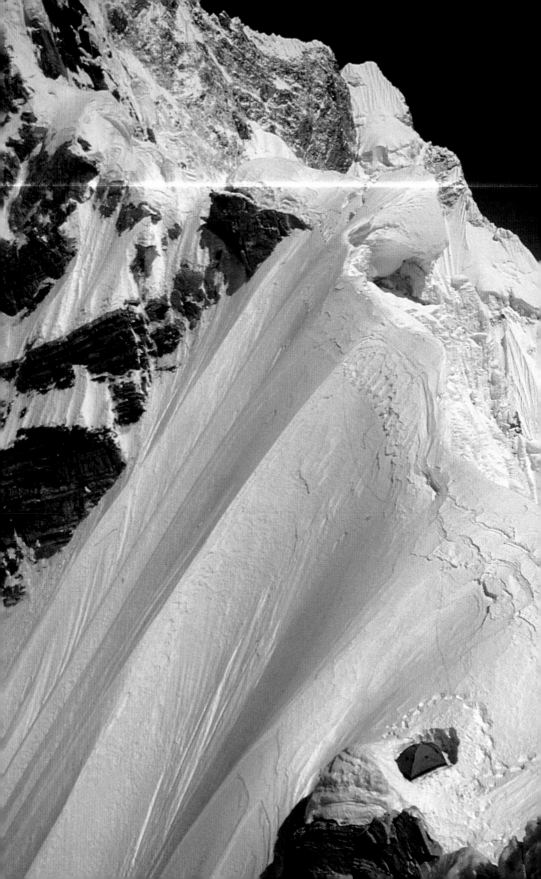

12
Camp 1

The missing porter loads were like a set of keys that you have put down in the wrong place. Just as you think you will go crazy at not being able to find them they turn up. Coming down into camp that evening from the climb we spotted a bright yellow sack at the end of the glacier. Whoever put it there had walked right past Advance Base Camp for half a mile. We were too tired to pick it up and decided to collect it the next morning. Peter MacPherson had also spotted a pile of sacks half a mile in the other direction, below camp, whilst picking up a load of his cine film from the 'lunch spot'. That left only two cases of gas unaccounted for. The others had traipsed in from Base Camp in the afternoon, and it was a relief to hear that the gas had been spotted, and marked, much further down the glacier. The problem with glacial moraine is that there are virtually no landmarks – one pile of boulders looks just like any other. Moraine may be bad for losing things in, but snow is worse. Leave a pair of crampons lying in the snow five feet from your tent and you are sure to lose them. If the afternoon sun does not heat them up and sink them without trace the evening snowfall will cover them over, and the problem then is one of memory. On an expedition to Kashmir I remember two friends leaving their crampons lying in the snow, and after excavating an area the size of several billiard tables to a depth of five feet they gave up in disgust.

Phuntso was the first to arrive that day. He was carrying an enormous load. He was only a small man, but with the strength of three. I think it must be the handfuls of chillies eaten with every meal that give hill men their strength. He also brought a request from Thimphu that Yeshey should return to Base Camp to speak to them on the radio. We were sorry to see him depart, but in any case he was suffering from conjunctivitis and needed to rest his eyes from the glare of the snow. Little did we imagine that events would prevent him returning to the mountain.

On 3 October five climbers set out again, determined to reach Camp 1. Al and Pete, aided by a very loud alarm clock which I think woke the whole camp up, got away early to set up their film gear near the base of the snow cone. What they really needed now was some climbing action, but lugging heavy cameras and tripods up the ramp was not a practical proposition, and Pete, who had had a bad fall in the moraine, was in pain with cracked ribs. The two hand-held cameras meant for shooting the climbing would be taken up only after we had established the tents and food stocks.

The dawn had long passed by the time I left camp, again behind Findlay and Lydia. A totally clear sky was deep blue through my dark goggles, and it was hot. Sweat soaked my back and ran down my face. The tip of my tongue felt sore where it had become burnt, unavoidable with one's mouth open, gasping all the time. I was developing the usual high-altitude cough, but it did not trouble me when I was moving, only if I stopped for more that a few minutes; then it was a hacking, irritating nuisance. I worried faintly that the chemicals in the constant stream of throat pastilles I was sucking would be doing me harm.

Coming up to the base of the snow cone I was hailed by Al: 'Hello, Mr Berry. How's it going? Who else is coming up today? Findlay and Lydia are about half an hour ahead of you; we filmed them just now. Hot, isn't it?'

I stopped, planted my axe in the snow, leant forward, resting my head on my forearm, and waited for my breathing to slow down. 'Too damned hot, Al. This snow will be really mushy by this afternoon. Jeff and Ginette are just back there, probably at the ice slope by now. You want to film something?'

Al had something in mind. 'Yes . . . well, what do you think? We hoped you might walk across that snow bridge for us, but don't worry mate. If you're not happy about it, don't do it.'

It was a good solid-looking bridge over a ten-foot-wide crevasse. I prodded the snow ahead of me with my axe before I went across. On the other side I yelled back, 'Good job it didn't collapse, Al. I'd be suing you for damages.' I waved them goodbye and, looking up at the climb, experienced a sharp feeling of despair at the thought of the steep, painful, repetitive climbing ahead. The right-hand rock buttress was still throwing a shadow and I followed in the steps of Steve and Lyd, close to the rock. Temperatures in the sun must have been in the eighties or nineties but there in the shade it was below freezing. Thin air – no radiation or convection, I thought. Pulling up the fixed ropes on the ramp, using one jumar and one axe, was so much easier than climbing in the normal way. After each exhausting set of steps I found I could rest all my muscles just by hanging in my harness from the jumar. The top section of rock and ice was the one section where I felt frightened – so steep that all my weight was hanging on the rope, with no chance of stopping if the rope broke or the jumar failed. This kind of fear is far easier to cope with than the fear of slipping and falling. Either the rope will hold or it won't, and if it doesn't there is nothing you can do about it. Once you've been on the rope for five minutes and it hasn't deposited you on the glacier below you get used to the idea that it's not going to.

On top of the orange rock, where we had dumped our loads I fell asleep in the sun for half an hour, though I kept jerking awake with no air in my lungs. I was finally woken by loud shouts in an American accent and Jeff and Ginette joined me, suitably impressed by the climbing so far. For a short time we watched Findlay and Lyd up in the top of the Jap gully pulling the Austrian fixed ropes out of the snow. Amongst the loads on the rock there was a large bag of nuts and raisins to dig into, and I was amused that the pair of choughs, now regularly seen at Advance Base Camp had not learnt the fact that climbers spell food; their well educated Nepalese cousins would have found a way into the bag by now.

I eventually caught up with Lydia at the very top of the Japanese gully. The slope steepened there, merging with a wall of rock. My jumar slid up the rope and the front points of my crampons bit the hard ice. Lyd was wedged into a constricted alcove in the rock, safeguarded by a couple of old Japanese pitons. She was waiting there for a shout from Findlay that it was safe for her to follow. He had disappeared round a blind corner, following the old fixed ropes, and now, no matter how hard we shouted together, there was no reply. Lydia fretted and finally decided to follow. I bade her good luck and she was gone.

I waited. Dark clouds were appearing from the north-west and my watch said 3.15 p.m. By the time Jeff and Ginette arrived it was obvious we could not risk following the other two to Camp 1; it would be dark by 6.30 p.m. In the extremely confined space we struggled to empty our sacks of the loads we had brought, and left them hanging, clipped on to the pitons. The fixed rope was a bitch. It had either shrunk or been tied off too tightly because try as I might I could not pull enough in to thread through my abseil device. With Ginette and me both pulling it was accomplished and I was off down to the safety and comfort of Advance Base Camp. I thought about Steve and Lydia and could imagine them having an epic time up there on the ridge in the gathering storm and darkness. There was no choice for them but to find a site for Camp 1 tonight.

Steve Findlay:

'I clipped into the old ropes and from the rock alcove teetered off left, my crampons scraping on the verglassed rocks. Ahead of me there was a vertical step with the faded ropes disappearing into the ice above. From where I was I could not see the rope re-emerge from the ice and had no way of knowing to what, if anything, it was attached. After pulling on it as hard as I could I decided to trust it, and transferred all my weight onto the jumar; it held. The rope had to be smashed out of the ice on many of the sections above; the terrain a mixture of steep rock and ice, with gullies filled with soft sugary snow. Lydia joined me halfway through the rocks and belayed on some Japanese pegs, festooned in old slings. Sometimes there were the sun-bleached Jap ropes as well as the purple Austrian lines, but only the Austrians' looked trustworthy. I thought they looked incongruous on this mountain where we were supposed to be out on a limb away from everyone. The mountain was no longer clean.

'Above us was a nasty little overhang; the rope had frayed a little where it had been rubbing on the lip. With a heavy sack and only one jumar the effort to surmount it was crucifying. Fifty more feet and we topped out on the ridge. It looked sharp and curved up into the cloud – huge drops on either side. We took turns plugging steps just below the crest of the ridge for another 500–600ft. Occasionally on the steep sections the crest would break, sliding away for ever to the glacier 2,500ft below. The weather was becoming rather unpleasant, with high winds and cloud, and time was pressing us to hurry. Instead of obeying my body to stop and rest regularly, in my worry to find a level place for the tent I forced myself to override the impulse, and as a result vomited several times from overexertion.

'For half an hour we searched in the lee of the ridge for a level spot, with no success, and eventually chopped out a six-by-three-foot platform on the slope itself, for our single-skin two-man tent. It was good to collapse into our pits and we slept for an hour before getting the brewing process under way. We had done what we set out to do and felt a heady euphoria that night in our tiny shelter.'

In the morning I looked up at the ridge through the large 600mm lens but could see no sign of a tent. Where were they? I guessed that they had probably pitched just the other side of the ridge, to get out of the wind. Other people were going up today; they would find out.

I spent most of the morning reading my half of Peter Fleming's *Brazilian Adventure*. With people desperate to read new books, they were being cut up into two parts, and just as I reached the exciting bit I found that the other half of the book had moved with its owner to Camp 1.

Around midday people in camp gathered round the lens and watched with excitement as a tiny dot emerged from the rock band above the Japanese gully and slowly crawled along the sharp snow arête of the south ridge proper. After an hour, two more dots appeared moving upwards, but shortly after that clouds closed in and we lost all sight of them.

Six and a half hours after leaving camp Steve Monks reappeared. He had been all the way to Camp 1 with a load. He confirmed that the tent was dug into the snow slope behind the ridge. For most of us the carry to Camp 1 was at least a nine-hour round trip, at the end of which we would be completely exhausted. Steve, though, showed none of the outward signs that he had been working to his limit for six and a half hours. He was still lively, grinning as usual, and had stomped into camp at the same pace as he had left it.

He told us he had met Findlay and Lydia, who were about to come down again, but he had managed to persuade them to stay at Camp 1 now that they had been resupplied with food and fuel. Tomorrow they would try to start the climb towards Camp 2.

Jeff was the next to appear stumbling out of the mist. He was able now to laugh off a potentially serious situation he had found himself in near Camp 1. He and Harry had been following the fixed ropes up the arête when the cloud had thickened. They came to the end of the roped section and could not see Camp 1. As there were no replies to their shouts, Jeff had gone ahead and in the white-out conditions he had wandered off the ridge. A real fear of walking right off the side of the mountain had taken him, and he had become seriously worried that he would not be able to find the fixed ropes again. Snow was falling, the temperature was freezing, and he could not see where he was going. He had been greatly relieved to find Harry again, and they had dumped their loads at the end of the fixed ropes.

I asked him how Harry had made out with the altitude, and sadly Jeff confirmed that 'H' had suffered all day with a racking, chesty cough. It was at that point, I think, that we all knew that Harry would not be going much higher. There was still a chance that his chest would improve – time would tell – but it seemed like a repeat of exactly the problem on Cho Oyu and several weeks at Base Camp there had not cured the complaint.

The weather was beginning to show signs of worsening. On 5 October Jeff and I set off at 6 a.m., but ominous dark clouds blotted out the sky and a few light flakes drifted down. Nevertheless, the cloud layer was high enough for us to see the western horizon, and we hoped that the rising sun would restore a blue sky. A thick layer of snow had fallen in the night and it had not frozen, as it would normally have done with a clear night sky.

We resolutely ploughed our way across the glacier, at every step sinking in a foot or so, but annoyance at the less-than-perfect conditions turned to exasperation and sheer frustration on the slopes of the snow cone, where each step was thigh-deep. If a step collapsed only frantic pedalling would stop a fall and avoid the uncomfortable experience of landing face down in the wet snow.

For Jeff this was the third day working in a row, and by the time he had joined me at the start of the fixed ropes he had had enough. Wishing me luck, he dumped his load and returned to camp.

By midday the weather had not improved; if anything it was more forbidding than at first light. It had taken me all that time to reach the orange rock at the top of the ramp. The effort had left me weakened to the extent that I could not face another upward step, and I too abandoned any idea of reaching Camp 1 that day. The descent was itself an ordeal. Frequently, whilst walking downhill, my feet would be unable to maintain the momentum set up by the upper half of my body and I would fall on my face, cursing. Snow had found its way in over the top of my gaiters, and my socks were now squelching. By the time I at last sat down at Advance Base Camp my feet felt raw. It was snowing by then, and Lydia and Findlay appeared in the early evening, needing to reacclimatise and sure the weather was changing for the worse. I secretly hoped that it would be snowing the next day, as I had promised to do a full carry to Camp 1.

View from Advance Base Camp

13
Tactical Withdrawal

It snowed all night and continued all the next day. A muffle of dense cloud enveloped the camp, and small flakes drifted down at the same consistent, gentle rate. Occasionally we could hear the distant roar of an avalanche scything down the west face, and then brooding silence returned again. We waited expectantly. This was not just a passing cloud, gone in an hour or two, but as yet there was not the slightest stirring of wind to herald a change for the better or for the worse.

The snow had built up round the tent during the night and pressed in against the walls. An hour or so after waking I was encouraged, by fairly violent prodding, to brave the cold outside and to shovel away the snow. In any case, my turn had come round again to cook breakfast. I emerged from my down sleeping bag, and, half crouching, I struggled into my Gortex shell waterproofs and plastic double boots. Putting up my down hood, I unzipped the inner and outer doors of the dome and squeezed out through the restricted doorway, floundering into the knee-deep snow outside. Light-hearted abuse followed me, because I had unavoidably shaken the tent upon leaving, showering Steve and Lydia with the condensation frozen on the inside.

After digging a trench round the tent I plodded over to the kitchen. Although the walls of the kitchen had been built, we were short of a roof. A tarpaulin and a couple of poles were due to come up from Base, but now it was too late – the kitchen was four feet deep in snow. In the sub-zero temperatures, I dug in the snowdrift for the petrol stove and the pots and pans from last night's dinner. The pans had not been cleaned and now the remains of supper was frozen solid. I chipped most of it off with a fish slice, and primed the stove, my fumbling fingers numb and clumsy. The stove was marginally better, now that Peter MacPherson had given it a service of sorts, but still it was troublesome. I knew that if my father could have seen this he would have laughed, as it had become a standing joke between us that one day I would learn the lesson of making sure I had the right stoves on an expedition. His own trip to Nun Kun in Kashmir in 1946 had suffered the 'stoves are knackered' problem, and he finds it hard to believe, forty years on, that the problem has not been solved. I was now paying the penalty of excessive thrift. I should have taken more high-altitude cooking gas, even though it was expensive to air-freight it separately.

I rigged an umbrella over the cooking area to keep off the worst of the falling white fluff, and then made my way down to the pond for water. I spilled half of it on the way back. I set the large metal pot down and, returning a minute later, was confused to find that it was empty; someone had made a small puncture in the bottom the previous day, chipping ice off with an axe.

Al and Pete emerged from their dome tent next to the kitchen to film the misery of life on a Himalayan expedition – specifically, me, up to my knees in snow, trying my best to perform the simple task of boiling some water.

Eventually the muesli and coffee were ready and I went from tent to tent handing it out. When I got to Monksie and Ginette's tent I was annoyed to find that Steve had purloined a gas stove and was using valuable gas, meant only for Camp 1 and above. There was a scuffle as I reached into the bell of their tent and retrieved the stove, Steve laughingly gave it up. If one tent started using gas, I reasoned, everyone would start using it. As it was we were all aware that sitting there at Advance Base Camp we were consuming food meant for the mountain. If this bad weather lasted any length of time the nine of us would very soon be making a significant inroad into our stocks. Even if it did improve immediately, the mountain would be out of condition for climbing until we had had a couple of fine days, with hard freezes in between, to consolidate the snow.

One day's bad weather, though, was not sufficient reason to drop back to Base, and in any case the journey back would be a dangerous and desperately tiring slog.

It was an enjoyable day in spite of the weather and I spent most of the time in Al and Pete's tent talking, and playing chess with Lydia. I discovered that Pete, like me, had been born just outside Calcutta and that his father had held a good position in a British company in India for thirty years. The company had suddenly been nationalised and as a result his father had lost nearly all the things he had worked so hard for.

Peter is a tall clean-shaven man in his mid-thirties, who Lydia and Ginette felt bore a close resemblance to Indiana Jones, though he often wore an expression that made him seem more serious than he was. He always appeared smart without being pretentious, and usually wore – even at Advance Base Camp – a well travelled trilby or the Peruvian equivalent of a balaclava. He was a freelance adventure cameraman and owned most of the film gear we had with us. The rest of the film team liked to pull his leg about his habit of sleeping with all his alloy boxes of film equipment piled around him, and for retaining a professional composure no matter what the situation. His film assignments had taken him to some outlandish places. He had filmed underwater in cave systems off Bermuda, covered hang gliding in the jungles of South America, and had some experience of filming serious climbing on a remote mountain in Alaska.

Pete showed Lyd and me how to operate and load cassettes into the compact clockwork 16mm cine camera which was for use at high altitude. I was intrigued to hear that it was the very same camera used by Joe Tasker to take the summit shots on a mountain in China called Kongur on the much publicised 1981 expedition led by Chris Bonington. We were also instructed how to thread film into a much larger and heavier camera called a Scupic, which Al wanted us to take up the mountain. I expressed my doubts on the practicality of using such a large, heavy camera whilst climbing, particularly because while loading it in a tent was one thing, threading film on a steep slope with gloves on was quite another. I was proved wrong, however, as the Scupic was used by Pete to film parts of the ramp later on.

In the evening Steve Findlay cooked for Al and Pete in our tent, having first gone to some trouble in preparing formal invitation cards. They arrived bearing gifts and Al had even engineered a dicky bow-tie from some piece of spare material. We got fairly plastered on Drambuie and in a happy blur we carried on rapping until well past our usual bedtime of 7 p.m.

Food is a main topic of conversation on an expedition and it is reassuring to know that everybody is suffering in equal amounts from the lack of those things taken so much for granted back home in the West. A favourite game was inventing the tastiest meal one could think of, and then teasing the others by saying, at a moment when it was least expected, 'You know, what I would really like now is a big plate of steak, mushrooms, chips, tomatoes and fried onions.' To which a standard reply would be: 'You bastard, Berry. I'd just managed to forget about the existence of steak in the universe. No supper for you tomorrow night, and I was going to give you boiled lobster in a wine sauce, with all the trimmings, followed by baked bananas in cinnamon-flavoured syrup, brandy and cigars.'

In fact, as far as our high-altitude food went, we were trying a new idea. We wanted to get away from the usual dehydrated or freeze-dried rations. Other Himalayan teams have lived on vegetarian diets, but what we had was a wholefood menu. A firm in Bristol, Nova Wholefoods Co-op, had carefully worked out for us a calorie-controlled diet of tasty, healthy, but light foods, which could be cooked easily and which we would look forward to eating. I am convinced that our continued strength and lack of digestion problems came from this change in approach. However, the purist ethic can be taken too far, and it has to be admitted that we took along canned meat and sugar.

After a day of gentle snow the bad weather deepened, and during the night gusting winds rattled our tents. By morning another foot of new snow lay over camp. The kitchen was now totally unmanageable and we cooked in our tents, on gas.

During the night my book had found its way into a puddle near my feet and dampness was also creeping into our clothes and sleeping bags. The heat from our prone bodies slowly but surely radiated through the floor of the tent, even though it was covered with sheets of thin Kariamatting and cardboard packing cases, and we each found that we were lying in shallow and uncomfortable depressions. We lay in the middle of an untidy, sordid pile of spare clothes, duvets, waterproofs and boots. The side pockets of the tent bulged with batteries, tape cassettes, lighters, candles, books and bog paper. With the stove going a cosy fug built up, but extreme caution was needed not to 'shit in one's own backyard', as Findlay so aptly put it. I suppose it was as smelly as a pigsty, but the human nose has a remarkable ability to adjust to any situation and I can't say I remember it being particularly bad. The piss bottle was emptied every morning of its foul yellow contents, its screw lid containing the odours that would have made the tent seem like a latrine. It is an unfortunate fact that, even if one remembers to have a piss before going to bed, nature calls at least once during the night. Again, extreme caution is required not to wake one's companions, or, kneeling in the dim light of a failing head torch, with several layers of bulky clothing to deal with, not to spray a friend's sleeping bag by mistake.

By 8 a.m. there were some signs of the wind and snow slackening, but the weather gave every appearance of being set foul for a while yet. Without a doubt we would be spending another day dossing in camp. As the hours wore on so opinion hardened that, whatever it was like tomorrow, we should force our way back down to Base Camp. We consoled ourselves with the thought that we would be able to bring back with us the stoves and food that the yaks were bringing from Bumthang.

On the night of 7 October the worst of the storm arrived, lashing the tents in earnest. The winds rose to gale force at 9.30 p.m. and there was not the slightest break in the screaming, howling madness right through the night and on until 10 a.m. the next morning. The tent became a wild thing of cracking, banging fabric whilst outside the mournful, incessant howl made me imagine that it was the very earth itself crying out in pain. At first I revelled in the storm's wild fury, shouting back at it to blow harder, but after a while, after the novelty had worn off, the cacophony of noise became an oppressive irritant and I slept only fitfully. I lay worrying whether Camp 1 and all our supplies on the ridge had blown away. In the strongest gusts the wall of the tent inverted, pressing down on my head, and fine particles of snow were being forced through a ventilation patch and fell on my upturned face. I snuggled up to Lydia, who before going to bed had torn me off a strip for teasing her at supper about her fancying Pete. Temporarily, I was not in her good books.

Just before midday on 8 October we strapped on snow shoes, turned our backs on Advance Base Camp and laboriously ploughed a furrow across the snow bowl. The sun appeared from time to time, but it gave no warmth, and occasional savage gusts whipped across the flat expanse, engulfing us in clouds of stinging snow particles.

Findlay and Lydia, on one of their earlier carries from Base, had climbed directly up into the snow bowl by taking a variation route through a small ice fall, where the tributary glacier merged with the main Mangde Chu ice flow. We had resolved to descend this way to avoid some of the potential danger of breaking bones on the snow-covered rocks. At the top of the ice fall a dozen or so crevasses gaped open, and we roped up for safety. The last one involved climbing down fifteen feet into the crevasse and jumping to a snow ledge on the other side. Beyond that the ice fall was safe and uncomplicated. The tributary glacier formed by the enormous snow bowl fell down the 700- or 800-foot slope to the main glacier in roller-coaster waves of ice, breaking up badly and forming dangerous seracs over to our right, but safe where we had chosen to descend. Three hours out from Advance Base Camp we found ourselves back on the treacherous moraine. I fell further and further behind the others and when I did finally top out on the other side there was Harry waiting for me as usual, with words of encouragement and some boiled sweets.

What bliss to be back in Base where the air seemed thick enough to breathe properly, and someone else was there to do the cooking!

We were greeted with happy enthusiasm by our Bhutanese friends and Mark and Chris as we stumbled the last few yards and ducked under the tarpaulin into the smoky kitchen. This time large mugs of coffee were waiting for us and Phuntso had cooked a huge evening meal of fried yak meat, rice, radishes, cabbage, carrots and chillies, followed by stewed pears, coffee and whisky. However, Base Camp was no longer the grassy meadow we had enjoyed upon arrival. There was now six inches of snow cover and it was as cold at night down there as it had been at Advance Base Camp.

Yeshey apologetically presented the bad news that the yaks had not arrived with our fresh supplies. We knew it was not his fault, and in any case I was not surprised: it was still only ten days since we had made our radio request. It had after all taken us nine days ourselves from Bumthang; perhaps they would arrive tomorrow.

The next day the yaks did not arrive. Looking up at the pass from camp it seemed to us that the snow was probably no worse than that which we had encountered across the glacier. We felt that they ought to get through.

In the afternoon I went to look for some snow leopard tracks that Mark had seen some way from the camp. I did not find them but was surprised by the number of other criss-cross trails in the snow made by smaller animals. One set were certainly from a padded foot – I imagine a smaller wild cat or a fox. Another track was like a zipper across the snow, something moving fast, perhaps a hare. There was plenty of evidence of wildlife but we rarely saw anything. I noticed that every morning, at dawn, a pair of large ravens came and landed on a rock near my tent. They never stayed long, though, just made their imperious croaking sound and flew off, to be replaced in mid-morning by a pair of equally black, smaller but much cheekier choughs, which had begun to realise that the rubbish tip was a source of scraps. Unlike the ravens, they were not too proud or frightened to eat from the tip, and I enjoyed the pleasure of listening to the pings of their aerial asdic.

The weather was definitely clearing up. It was sunny at Base Camp, though Gangkar Punsum was still moth-balled in a large mass of cloud. We washed our dirty clothes and shampooed our greasy, matted hair, using hot water from the kitchen. We were enjoying to the full the luxuries of Base Camp.

We decided to stay one more day in the hope that the yaks would turn up with the things we needed, and to allow the weather to improve sufficiently to permit us to start climbing again. Jeff and Ginette were impatient to get back up again. Lydia had developed an infected throat and was happy not to aggravate it by more heavy work too soon, but she surprised me with the news that Yeshey had told her that he did not want to do any more climbing. I was shocked by this and went to talk to him. I was mystified when he offered no reasons other than not liking our food and feeling that the time was not right. There was something here I had not understood and I reflected on the problem overnight.

Here was a man proud to be the best climber in his country, with four expeditions already to his credit, his highest ambition to climb his country's highest peak, and yet he was not keen to climb with us. Why? I saw it as my fault. I had not made enough effort to ensure that he became our friend. All he had faced so far were problems – the shortage of rations, Al's heavy-handed criticism of the staff, the lost loads on the glacier, the fact that he had ended up in Al and Pete's tent instead of being in with the climbers themselves at Advance Base Camp. By nature he was a reserved, mild-mannered, civilised man and I felt that he had begun to believe that he was not entirely welcome, but was too polite to say anything. Added to that there was probably the human problem that all climbers suffer from, the 'let's stay in the café' syndrome.

Now that he was back with Gopa and Tobgay and the others at Base, with plenty of chillies to eat, the idea that he would always be able to come back again in the future was sapping his resolve. Selfishly, I also wondered whether on our return to Thimphu it would reflect badly on the expedition that Yeshey had refused to climb with us.

Next morning I privately broached the subject with him again: 'Yeshey, we are all very sorry you are staying at Base; we honestly just want you to be our friend – you know, to really be one of us, and help us with the climb. You're really strong and we do need your help, and everyone was really impressed by your climbing that day we climbed the ramp. Won't you change your mind? We really do want you to come with us.'

'Oh, yes, thank you, Berry la, but I think I'll come here again. There is plenty of time for me to do this.'

'Look, I know you don't like our food, Yeshey, but we can take some of the stuff from here for you. We are going to climb this mountain. Come with us. Just think – you'll be famous in your country; you'll be in all the history books.' We laughed together at this, and I went on: 'I'm sorry about all the trouble you have had to deal with, but we're all grateful for your efforts in trying to sort it out. Please think about it for a while, Yeshey. It would be really good to have you along.'

'Yes, I'll think about it – and thank you, Berry la.'

At lunch time Yeshey sought me out and told me that he was happy to come back with us. I was pleased, but in some quarters my action was not greeted enthusiastically. I should have left him to make up his own mind and not put him under pressure, Lydia said. I felt hurt by these remarks. As it was, I was all too conscious that my action to persuade him would rest heavily on my mind if ever there was an accident. He had a wife and child back in the capital. But would he not regret not coming with us once we had conquered Gangkar Punsum? Surely that was what he wanted, and weren't we the obstacle preventing his joining in? Would not his friends and countrymen think he had failed or, worse, think that he was a coward for abandoning his attempt?

The second day at Base passed slowly with still no sign of the yaks. We knew that they had left Bumthang; we could only think that there had been some hold-up at the change-over at the hot springs.

It needed someone with authority to go and sort out whatever the problem was. The young mail-runner boy who was coming back with them, I felt, would not command enough respect to deal with the tough yak herders. I tackled Yeshey and Gopa on the subject, suggesting that Gopa should make the journey to discover what had happened. Stalling, he and Yeshey said that they felt confident that the yaks would definitely arrive the following day.

Amongst ourselves we decided that it was unnecessary, and a waste of food and gas, for everyone to return to Advance Base Camp together. Monksie, Ginette, Harry and Jeff would go back the next day, with the intention that two people would move up and live at Camp 1, pushing out the route to Camp 2. The other pair would finish the load-carrying to Camp 1. Then in a couple of days Findlay, Lydia, myself and Yeshey would go and take over the climbing beyond Camp 1 and move the supplies across the 'dinosaur' ridge to Camp 2, while whoever needed to rest could do so at Advance Base Camp.

Accordingly, on the following morning of 11 October, the others plus Peter headed back to Advance Base Camp. We were later to discover that Pete had slipped whilst crossing the moraine, fallen heavily, and was now suffering from two suspected cracked ribs. Apparently, by late afternoon, when he had failed to turn up in camp, one of the others had gone in search of him and had found him propped against a boulder, asleep. He could not even remember stopping and thought he must have been suffering from mild shock.

Base Camp was practically clear of snow again with this the third day in a row of sunny weather. Gangkar Punsum herself was now free of storm, the prevailing north-west wind whipping snow off her summit ridges. Each afternoon a cloud the size of the mountain itself would be formed to the south of the massif by the drop in pressure as the wind, straight from Tibet, swirled past the mountain. Clear night-time skies brought hard freezes, spelling good conditions for high on the peak. I was becoming impatient to be up there taking part in the climbing.

By the late afternoon on the 11th not a solitary yak had appeared and, sitting down with Yeshey and Gopa again, I insisted that Gopa should set off the next day to unravel the mystery of the disappearing yaks. I was also concerned that we were not living up to our promises of sending regular reports to BBC TV news and

Above *Dr Ginette Harrison on the cornices of the 'Dinosaur' ridge. (Photo: Steven Berry)*

Below *Nearing the snow dome while descending from Camp 2. (Photo: Steven Berry)*

Overleaf *Masked dancer at the King's birthday celebrations. (Photo: Steven Berry)*

BBC Radio, and wanted Gopa to carry our film and tape reports for onward transport. However, he was genuinely worried about making the journey on his own because of the 'many wild animals' and politely, but firmly, insisted that Yeshey accompany him. I relented, as by now we were really quite low on food at Base Camp. Yeshey promised to return to the mountain as soon as he possibly could.

On 12 October they set off and it was not until the end of the climbing that I discovered what had happened. It was as well that Yeshey had gone with Gopa, who would probably not be alive today but for that decision. At the top of the pass the conditions had been atrocious, thigh-deep drifts all but halting their progress. They decided to press on even though the path, vague as it had been, was now hidden under the snow. They became lost and spent two nights in the open with only one sleeping bag between them. To their surprise they found that there was snow all the way down to the pass before the hot springs. It took them five days just to reach Dur Sachu. This was why the yaks had not come through; their handlers had refused to take them above the snow line with nothing for them to graze on.

At dinner on the fourth night we debated heatedly what we should do next. I wanted to get back and help the others with the climbing. In total our budget stretched to a maximum of a month of climbing and every day was beginning to count. If the yaks arrived the next day or the day after, Yeshey knew what we needed and was capable of organising Phuntso and some of the lads to porter it over. We no longer needed to stay here and, I argued, it was more likely that we would be of use at Advance Base Camp. Findlay wavered between agreeing with me and agreeing with Lydia and Al, who wanted to stay one more day. They pointed out that no one had yet been seen climbing to Camp 1, and therefore we were probably not needed yet. What did one more day matter in the circumstances? The discussion ended in no conclusion, and we retired to Findlay's tent for a marathon session at cards. Steve, not playing himself, showed remarkable tolerance, making not a hint of complaint as we carried on our noisy game until well past midnight.

At breakfast I asked what people had decided to do. 'We're going to stay here one more day, Steve,' Findlay replied.

West Ridge

Gangkar Punsum (24,770ft)

1985 Japanese High Point

Dinosaur Ridge

Snow Dome

Last point reached

Camp 2 (22,000ft)

Camp 1 (20,500ft)

Note: **Summit pyramid vastly foreshortened**

View of Gangkar Punsum taken from the north-west

'Well, OK, that's up to you, but I'm going back today,' I replied, feeling some anger and frustration that I couldn't change their minds. I felt strong crossing the glacier; the rest at Base had undoubtedly done me good. Six hours later I was being served tea and listening to the story of Pete's cracked ribs and the other news in camp.

14
The Dinosaur

I squatted at the entrance to Pete's tent, my hands wrapped round a metal cup of hot soup, and listened intently as he first related the story of his fall in the moraine – he had banged his head badly, smashed his glacier glasses and possibly cracked two ribs – and then to the better news that earlier on the day of my arrival he had seen Monksie and Jeff moving up the ridge to occupy Camp 1. The previous day, the four climbers had tried to get through to Camp 1 but the snow conditions had been too bad for all but the final section of the snow cone and they had been forced to turn back. Harry, apparently, had taken a big fall on the descent, but was uninjured, and had gone back up today, with Ginette, carrying a load.

Harry McAulay:

'We had taken our crampons off earlier, when the snow was soft, and had set off down the steep slopes from the top of the snow cone without them. Jeff was in front, back-heeling, setting a rapid pace. Monks came past me at great speed, and I decided to go faster to keep up with them. They were making it look so damned easy, and if they could do it then so could I – an attitude which in this case was to be my downfall. I can remember that the instant my heels hit ice the words Monks had spoken earlier during a discussion on self-arrest came back into my mind: "Harry, I shouldn't think that on slopes as steep as this self-arrest with an axe would stop you."

'He was right. My heels went from under me and I started falling. The axe was wrenched from my grasp as my speed increased, my heels momentarily dug in but served only to cartwheel me down the slope. I glimpsed the rocks at the side of the snow cone and hoped I wouldn't hit them. Time seemed frozen. I calmly wondered what it would be like to hit rocks at this speed. I worried about being impaled by the axe, fastened to my wrist by a length of tape; there was nothing I could do about it. I kept thinking what a burk I was to have fallen. I fell three or four hundred feet and when I finally came to a stop, my goggles full of snow, I had suffered only bruises.'

I determined to do a carry myself to Camp 1 the next day. I lay in bed that night wondering what the section beyond the Jap gully was going to be like. Those who had done it had said that it made the rock and ice at the top of the ramp seem child's play in comparison. Although I was tired from the glacier crossing, my excitement and nervousness would not allow sleep to come. I would be on my own tomorrow. Then, just as reality faded away unnoticed, the enormous roar of an avalanche brought me bolt upright. It sounded so close, yet I knew that here we were perfectly safe. I settled down again. It must have been in the Jap gully.

At 6.20 a.m. I was hoisting my heavy rucksack on to a boulder. I turned, sank down and slipped my arms through the straps, grunting with the effort as I rose to my feet. I was away, the others still fast asleep. The tips of the peaks to the west were smudged pink in the dawn. It was going to be a clear day. Slow as the coming day seemed, I knew that unless I hurried I would be caught on the snow cone and the ramp in the baking heat. If I could stay in shadow I would be much faster than out under the onslaught of the sun. Better cold than fried, I thought.

For once I did not feel drugged by sleep. I felt confident, happy, like a runner in a race when he knows he has the opposition beaten. Ten minutes later out of bed and the sun would have beaten me to it. As I moved steadily upwards the edge of the shadow chased my heels. However, I paid the price of my choice. As I stood at the beginning of the Jap gully I had to work hard to restore life to my left hand. It had frozen through three layers of gloves – I had been holding the metal head of the ice axe as I came up the ramp. Now the pain was almost unbearable as the circulation returned. I cried openly – after all, there was no one to see or hear me.

At the top of the Jap gully, in the rock alcove, I checked my gear a second time and tried to relax my nerves. Over my shoulder I pushed my axe down between my rucksack and my back, leaving my left hand free. My right gripped the jumar, clipped to the old Austrian rope which disappeared round the corner. I checked again the sling connecting the jumar to my harness, unclipped from the belay, and swung round.

One moment there was the comfortable safety of the Jap gully beneath me, the next I was hanging on the rope with a 2,000ft drop below to the glacier at the foot of the west face. I looked up. The tatters of the original Jap rope, bleached white in the sun, with the newer purple Austrian rope beside it, snaked up and out of sight through a jigsaw of vertical rock buttresses and narrow, ice-filled gullies. The 7mm rope looked horribly thin and was badly frayed in two places where it passed over rough granite edges. 'Don't think about it, just do it,' I said to myself. I passed half a dozen places where the rope was tied into the old Japanese pegs, requiring patient, careful change-overs from one rope to another. Two rock sections in particular are etched indelibly on my memory. Vertical, with me leaning out, pulling with all my strength on the jumar, placing the points of my crampons on tiny holds to give enough purchase to pull up another few feet. The memory of the crucifying pain of the effort involved has faded now, but I do recall thinking nothing could be worse. I remember also talking to myself, rambling nonsense, just anything that came into my head. It helped to encourage me, perhaps took my mind off the danger, or the pain. My altitude cough was a lot worse, I spat out large lumps of green phlegm, my throat felt septic. There was that feeling that if I coughed hard enough I'd get rid of the infection in one go. Instead, I retched so badly that I thought I might be sick.

The ropes continued up the ridge, though the previous day's steps had been filled by the wind. Plod, plod, plod, ten steps rest, fifteen steps rest. The cloud moved in and the wind started to pick up. Light snow started to drive into my left side, and on the stronger gusts I had to stop and brace myself. The fixed rope was coated in ice and as I slid the jumar up the rope and pulled, it frequently would not grip. I would have to stop, unclip the clamp, and breathe on the iced-up cam until the grippers were free of ice, being careful at the same time not to let my lips touch the frozen metal. Just as I was worrying about making the same mistake as Jeff, and not finding Camp 1, I saw Monksie appear out the mist above me. The wind was now moaning over the ridge and his words were torn away. He gestured to me to follow him and disappeared to my right.

Camp 1 (20,500ft) was a two-man tent on a small platform that had been carved out of a 40-degree snow slope. It was pitched fifty feet off the main ridge, as far away from where the wind whistled over the crest as possible. Jeff appeared shortly after me and we exchanged warm, shouted greetings. 'Berry, sahib, good to see you. What is in the mail-bag today? Any goodies? Now, look here my man, when are the lead climbers getting the Mars bars?' He was referring to a case of Mars bars we had reserved for summiteers. Jeff pouted, creased his forehead, and pointed a finger in mock sternness. I laughed. Trust him to play the clown, even in these conditions. 'Seriously, did Harry give you a list of stuff we need up here? I gave it to him yesterday,' he added.

'Yeah, I've got most of it, Ginette's got the rest. She's a half-hour behind, I think. I brought you a dome tent, you'll be pleased to hear. Jesus, I'm knackered! That top section is a killer. Hey, I didn't like the look of those frayed bits. Don't you think we should change them?'

'Yes, they're not good, but I expect they're OK. If you want to change them, why don't you do it on the way down?'.

I had thought about it myself, but not in these conditions. 'No, not today. I'm off as soon as I can before this weather gets any worse. Anyway, what I want to hear is, what have you two been up to? Did you get to Camp 2 today?' I unloaded the rucksack whilst Monksie inside the tent put on a brew.

'Nope, 'fraid not, the wind was too strong by the time we got up to the snow dome. But we could see all along the 'dinosaur' ridge. Probably another day should do it. It's wild up there, man. You wait till you see the cornices, you'll shit your pants.' We laughed. 'Hey, you'll never guess what we found. Just up below the snow dome there's a half-buried Austrian tent, and inside. . . .'

'Yeah, what?' I asked.

'A bunch of grub, some gas and a burner, pots and pans, and some cine film.'

'Wow, that's brilliant!' The disappointment that Camp 2 had not been reached was now offset by the thought that at least gas would no longer be a worry. It was cold now that I was not moving and I was anxious about the weather.

'OK, I'm off, then. When do you want some more people up here?'

Monksie spoke from the tent: 'Why don't you come up soon, Steve? Have a rest and we'll let you know when you're needed on the walkie-talkie. We're OK right now, but we'll be moving over to stay at Camp 2 once we've fixed the ropes across the 'dinosaur'.'

I put my empty sack back on, picked up my axe, and waved goodbye. Out on the ridge the conditions had produced practically a white-out. The cloud had become so thick that it was almost impossible to differentiate between cloud and snow; all idea of the angle of the slope had disappeared, except that I could still make out the holes in the snow made by my ice axe on the way up, and, for a few feet, I could see the rope leading downwards.

Rope length after rope length I side-stepped down the ridge, clipped to the rope by the caribiner on my harness, one arm twisted round the rope behind me, allowing it to slide slowly through my gloved hand. Where was Ginette? I should have met her by now. Just as I arrived at the top of the rocks I saw her blue helmet appear out of the mist. She looked up and gave me the pleasure of her pretty grin. I waited on the small platform, where the ropes disappeared into the ice, presumably tied to an Austrian 'dead man'. Quickly and efficiently we effected the change-over, exchanging news, and then I was abseiling down the rock. In between some of the belays the rope had been tied off so tight that I couldn't pull in enough slack to thread my descendeur. All I could possibly do was put one twist through the caribiner on my harness and wind one arm round the taught rope behind me, keeping a very careful eye on the rope passing through the 'crab'. I had visions of the rope passing over the screw gate and locking it so tight that I wouldn't be able to undo it, and then having to somehow cut myself off the rope without falling into the void.

Back in the Jap gully the fear vanished. I was on comparatively safe ground again. Relief, relief – time to smile again. Once below the ridge the wind had died, and now that I had emerged from the bottom of the cloud layer I could see Advance Base Camp. It was still snowing but I wasn't worried about that. The problem was that I was falling asleep on my feet. My head nodded, my arms hung down, the action in my legs was automatic, I couldn't even be bothered to take off my crampons at the foot of the ice slope. I felt so thirsty – the water bottle had frozen – and when I finally hit camp I drank two cups of vegetable soup, one cup of beef and tomato, and a cup of warm orange juice.

Over the next two days confidence that within a week we would be going for the summit was turned to worry that our progress was so slow that we wouldn't have time to climb the hardest sections of the route. Behind Camp 2 was the 200-foot rock buttress that the Japs had taken two days to climb, and near the summit was a similar buttress but about twice the size. On the 7 p.m. radio call each night we listened to Monksie's description of impossible gale force winds on the ridge. I went through the budget wondering exactly how many days we had left. Would the Bhutanese charge us for the days lost at Thimphu, Bumthang and the hot springs and the day waiting for the yaks to catch up, two days from Base Camp? I juggled with the possibilities and figured that to be safe we really needed to be leaving Base Camp on 3 November, which gave us roughly two weeks. Time enough, provided the weather improved.

Steve Findlay, Lydia and Al arrived at Advance Base Camp with the news that the yaks had still not appeared. It no longer worried me unduly: our food stocks would last two weeks and the life of a gas canister was proving to be better than we had assumed in our original calculations, and we also had the Austrian cans.

Al was becoming increasingly worried that he was not obtaining film of the real climbing. Pete's ribs were too painful for him to contemplate the climb to Camp 1, though originally he had aimed to reach Camp 2. Steve Findlay and I had both used the small clockwork cameras on previous climbs and the plan had been that we would use them to film above Camp 2.

On the morning of 17 October, as Findlay and I were packing to leave, Al shouted from his tent, 'Steve, are you taking the Scupic up today?'

'No, Al. Lydia's agreed to bring it up tomorrow.'

'Fucking hell, Steve, sometimes I don't think you care a toss about this film. You know I appreciate that the climbing gear is more important, but you've got what you need up there for now. Why can't you take the Scupic?'

Al hadn't spoken to me like this before, but it was early in the morning and I thought he was getting his knickers in a twist about nothing. It took me by surprise as well, and all I could manage was a feeble reply: 'Al, look, Lydia will definitely bring it up tomorrow. I'm taking a lead rope and some more gas, which is needed. OK?' So saying, I stormed off to Harry's tent for some spare head-torch batteries.

I explained what had happened, and added: 'Damn! I don't see why we should be expected to carry his gear up there, he can damn well carry it himself. I dare say he'll eat the food we've carted up there – if he ever comes to Camp 1, that is. I mean, he's just as strong as us why shouldn't he do his fair share? There's nothing in the contract about carrying all his food, tentage, film and cameras. It makes me mad.'

'Steve, if he was so concerned about the Scupic going up, then why hasn't he pressed us before now? The bloody thing has been here for three days,' Harry rejoined.

'Yes, I hadn't thought of that. I'll go and point it out to him.'

'Be tactful. Don't fly off the handle, mind, and look, he probably wants you to take it because he's worried that he won't make it up there himself, and it's obvious Pete won't.'

I walked back to the dome near the kitchen and called in: 'Don't worry about the Scupic, Al. Lyd will bring it. Besides, it's been here three days, hasn't it? In any case, I'm taking one of the clockwork cameras with me today. Anyway, why don't you come up? It's a beautiful dawn.'

Silence. He was obviously feeling aggrieved. The previous night we had promised him that the Scupic would go up today, with Lydia, but she had decided on another day's rest.

A curt 'No thanks' was all the response I was getting. Such is life. No matter how good a friendship may be, rows will always occur. Without doubt the expedition was marked by its happy relations and misunderstandings of this sort were a rare event.

Findlay kept me company, doing one more carry before moving up to Camp 1 himself. It was a beautiful day and the squabble with Al was soon forgotten; optimism returned with the advent of seemingly perfect weather. The climb went smoothly, and this time I was full of enthusiasm: today was not just another carry; I would be staying at Camp 1; tomorrow I knew I would be climbing higher. At 8 a.m., as we were nearing the snow cone, there was a sharp crack – the start of a large avalanche nearby. We swung round and watched as it thundered down the Jap gully from the hanging seracs, spilling out in a large cloud on to the snow bowl. We congratulated ourselves at being right not to have succumbed to the easy option of following the Japanese route in the first place.

Nearing Camp 1 the winds were again strong on the ridge, but with no cloud the panorama was magnificent. We looked down on the whole of Bhutan to the south of us, the low country a dark line seen over the tops of a broad belt of white peaks. I could just make

127

out the dark shape of the Black Mountains, the other side of Tongsa. On the far western border we could see a mountain much higher than the rest, Chomolhari (23,997ft), the peak F. Spencer Chapman had climbed in 1937. I knew it to be 80 miles distant. Beyond that again, 150 miles away, in the purple haze on the far horizon, a smudge of white *had* to be Kanchenjunga, the third highest mountain in the world, first climbed by that famous British rock climber Joe Brown and various friends in 1955. Gangkar Punsum herself blocked out our view to the east, but what I found so fascinating was that all the highest peaks were connected to her by one continuous ridge, spreading westwards, as sharp a border between the Tibetan plateau and the Indian subcontinent as any river would be in dividing two countries. It must have been exactly on this line that the two tectonic plates collided with each other a mere 20 million years ago, starting the creation of the Greater Himalaya.

When Findlay and I arrived at Camp 1 we found Steve Monks inside the newly erected dome feeling vaguely sick and lethargic. Jeff and Ginette had left early that morning to try yet again to get across to Camp 2. They returned in mid-afternoon, having been forced to turn back when almost there by increasing winds. However, they had fixed rope along a major section of the 'dinosaur' and were sure that this time one more day really would do it.

From my diary – 18 October

'Went with Monks to try to fix it to Camp 2. Left early hoping we'd miss the high winds, but no such luck! I've never known anything like it, clear sunny day, but on the ridge 60–70 m.p.h. wind. Very cold, even with all three pairs of gloves on – cold hands. Wearing thermal underwear, polar trousers, overtrousers, padded jacket, down duvet, silk balaclava, cricket hat, duvet hood over – just warm enough, feet cold but not freezing.

'Up the long ridge to the top of the first snow dome, a few steep bits on the way. At Austrian tent SM picked up 500ft fixing rope. First view of summit for some time, looks so close. Carry on over two more humps, again steep front-pointing bits, and then ahead is the 'dinosaur' ridge. Incredibly impressive with huge cornices. SM gaining on me. Wind so strong you stop, hoping it will relent – it doesn't. Take ten steps, try to regain breath, constant battle to stay upright.

'Communication by shouting in each other's ear. Face freezing. We carry on; I'm now seriously worried for my life. The ridge is getting very thin, could get blown off, stop moving and we'll freeze. We stop and decide to go back, nothing accomplished. SM worried about his feet – both dead. He, as usual, leaves me behind, back to warm his feet. Desperate business going down the ropes. Too much drag on them to pull enough through to put the descendeur on, so just clip into the screw gate and trust you don't trip over the crampons and go head first down the slope.

'Discussion in evening. I suggest all four of us go over, two to stay (Jeff and me), two to fix the last bit. Agreed.'

The next day Jeff and I knelt next to each other at the top of the snow dome, watching Steve and Ginette edge slowly along the 'dinosaur'. The wind had certainly slowed; maybe it was only 30–40 m.p.h. – strong enough to make life difficult but not devastating. There was not a single cloud from horizon to horizon, clear blue sky, yet still it blew. What made this continual wind, I wondered. Why did it never stop?

From the dump of equipment and food, dug into the side of the slope and marked with a ski stick, we pulled out what we would need to stay at Camp 2. A two-man tent, climbing rope, a snow shovel, a box of gas and a burner, some rock pegs and ice screws, caribiners and slings, some cine film for the Bolex autoload camera which I had in a carrying pouch strapped round my waist, and enough food for three days. We split the load between us, adding it to the personal gear and sleeping bags we were already carrying, and we knelt, waiting.

We had calculated that the snow dome was probably 22,000ft or a little higher, and from our elevated position Jeff and I looked across and slightly down on the 'dinosaur'. This section of the ridge was about half a mile in length and ended at the foot of the first rock buttress. Looking at it, I was reminded of a description I had once heard of a cliff in Wales. The climber concerned, propped against a bar in Llanberis, had described the cliff by saying, 'It was so steep that it was vertical one side and overhanging on the other.' This impossible description was almost a reality, with enormous cornices the full length of the ridge and the near-vertical north-western flank on the other.

We had given Steve Monks and Ginette a good head start from

129

Camp 1, and now they were almost at the far end of the ridge – two tiny dots, dwarfed by the size of the cornices on their right. We could just pick out Steve in his blue wind suit in the lead, whilst Ginette was sitting belaying him. He was trying to keep as far away from the cornices as possible in case they broke off, but the almost vertical nature of the north-western flank forced him to stay all the time close to the edge. Approximately every hundred feet he would sink a dead man into the slope and clip in the fixed rope. After a night's freeze the anchors would be immovable, but today they would need to be treated with caution. Steve's progress became slower and slower as he neared the end, but as we watched anxiously he topped the final rise in the ridge and waved both his hands over his head to signal to us that he could see the site for Camp 2.

I clipped my jumar on to the rope and followed Jeff. The fixed rope was being blown into the air in big arcs between each anchor, and I found that I had to pull the rope down in order to slide the jumar along. It was obvious to each of us that the rope was no more than something to hang on to, a psychological aid. If a cornice broke away and someone was left hanging on the rope on the other side of the ridge the chances of getting out again were realistically nil. Even a fall down the northern side offered only a slim chance of recovery.

At least there were someone else's footsteps to use. However, each step had to be taken carefully, and in some places, where the snow had the consistency of sugar, the steps had a tendency to collapse. Occasionally I took out the cine camera to film Jeff, but there was something wrong with the sound it was making; I concluded later that the mechanism was slightly frozen. The further along the ridge the more difficult and dangerous it became. On the far side of one rise was a drop to the next part of the ridge necessitating down-climbing a short wall of 70-degree snow, and further along, straddled on the ridge itself, we came to another drop of fifteen feet which involved what I can only describe as a thrashing slide. The worst section, though, without a doubt, was traversing along a thin, friable cornice. It was only about thirty feet long, but surviving from one side to the other was purely in the hands of fate. There was no alternative but to climb on the cornice itself. In parts our hands were actually on the top of the snow mushroom, and we could see the undercut base of the cornice underneath. I am sure that in everyone's life there are situations, even if you don't believe in God, where prayer is the last and natural resort. The friable cornice section was like that for me. I prayed out loud every time I went across it: 'Dear God, oh please don't let this collapse. Just let me get to the other side. I promise to try and be a better person in future. I know that doing this is very stupid, but I really don't want to die just yet. There are other things I have to do first. Please don't let this break away.'

Finally Jeff and I stood on the last rise looking down on a small gap in the ridge. From the notch a gully dropped down the northern side, funnelling the wind through the gap. Next to the notch was a rock lump behind which a snow bank offered the chance of digging in and getting a place out of the wind. Beyond Camp 2 the first 200ft rock buttress loomed vertically. We could see the remains of the Jap fixed ropes flailing in the wind. They certainly would not be safe to use, I thought. I was thoroughly exhausted and my attempts at digging a platform for the tent were short-lived; Jeff took over. We had made it to Camp 2, but that night, as we lay ensconced in our two-man Gortex shelter, the wind built back up to hurricane force.

15
The Winter Wind

Inside the single-skin lightweight tent there was enough room for two people to lie down but barely sufficient headroom to sit up. To make our cramped conditions worse we had, unknowingly, brought the one tent which had not been made with a bell-end for cooking, though cooking inside did give the illusion of heat for short periods in the day.

By the time darkness fell the maelstrom outside had developed into a high-pitched continuous howl. The wind shrieked up the gully and blasted through the gap right past our tent. Had we not found that one place behind the rock we would certainly have been plucked up and flung over the ridge. As it was, the side of our tent nearest the gully thrummed with an incessant, vibrant throbbing. The noise from the wind and the flapping tent was so loud that we had to raise our voices by several decibels to be understood.

It was a painfully uncomfortable night. Jeff sensibly had a Thermorest (a thin air mattress) as well as his foam Kariamat. In my efforts to cut down on weight I had dispensed with the former, and severely regretted it. For once I was cold all night; with no thin foam layer as a floor for the tent, as at Advance Base Camp or Camp 1, or cardboard packing cases, there was insufficient insulation. My feet were especially cold, even though in the middle of the night I wrapped them in a spare woollen shirt. The floor had hard bumps in all the wrong places, and we were so cramped that there just was not enough room to curl up. I twisted this way and that but it only added to the frustration. It was no good either hoping or thinking that the loud, oppressive din outside would stop. It could not be turned off like a record one has grown tired of, or turned down because it was too loud. Because of our new altitude – 22,000ft – anything involving lifting one's body, like having a piss in the bottle, was an exhausting effort. Having a shit involved the worst procedure of all – a task that was left until it could no longer be ignored. In the thirty-six hours that the hurricane wind continued to blow I only went outside on two occasions, and only for the said purpose. In our snow bank there was just enough room to crouch outside the tent door, ice particles blowing everywhere, and after the operation I scooped up the offending waste on the snow shovel, threw it into the gully and watched as it was then sent into orbit over the ridge.

Once the sun was up some warmth returned, however, and life was almost enjoyable again. After some soup for breakfast, I settled down with half of a Jack Higgins thriller, transported into a world of spies and intrigue. When I had finished, annoyed this time that the climax of the novel was at Advance Base Camp, we played cards until we could face no more, and then whiled away the long hours talking and eating. I wasted some film recording Jeff melting some ice for a brew. We were bored and it was something to do. Mostly we just talked.

Jeff and I had first met in America, when with separate partners we had made a 3½-day ascent of one of Yosemite valley's big-wall climbs. During those days of hot sunshine as we climbed higher and higher we egged each other on, shouting Anglo-American racial abuse at each other and thereby forming a firm friendship. Sometimes you know instinctively if another person is one hundred per cent dependable. I saw that in Jeff, and when he told me he was going to college to become a paramedic, and to specialise in mountain medicine, the thought had crossed my mind that he could be a useful person on a Himalayan expedition. A couple of years later the expedition to Cho Oyu needed a medical officer and so I rang him in America. Without hesitation he accepted the offer.

Thirty-six hours in a cold, cramped tent, at altitude, with the added irritant of the non-stop flapping noise, would be enough with most people to cause friction, but a more laid-back companion than Jeff would be hard to imagine. After being awake most of the first night I resolved not to allow myself to sleep during the day, in the hope that I would be so tired by nightfall that sleep would come easily, and far from having to tolerate someone else's presence I thoroughly enjoyed Jeff's banter and political comment. He has the young American's political awareness and can criticise the faults in the American system. His serious side, though, is vastly overshadowed by his extrovert nature. I envy him his natural ability to create fun wherever he goes. The Bhutanese loved him, as he related directly to their own irrepressible impish natures. They were highly amused by his outrageous T-shirts and his helicopter hat (a peaked hat with a propellor on the top). I admire also the way Jeff has not lost sight of normal values, working as he does as an ambulanceman in the gambling town of Reno, where every day he has to deal with a continual stream of human tragedy from drug addicts to suicides. Once he even had to attend a man having a heart attack in a brothel! He has only one habit which we all condemned in unison – chewing tobacco. Particularly revolting was the fact that during a chew he would, if in a tent, periodically spit filthy liquid into a cup. However, on this trip he had brought only one can of baccy in an effort to kick the habit, and he had run out by the time we were cut off at Camp 2. I cannot recall one instance when he lost his temper, and we enjoyed many hours during that time at Camp 2 discussing our futures, the future of the world and, more immediately, the next few days.

Jeff favoured an attempt on the rock buttress when the wind died, whereas I now felt that we had a better chance of the summit if we traversed below the buttress for a distance of 1,000ft, on steep hard ice, to reach a series of four interconnected ice slopes leading to the top. The disadvantage of my idea was that we would have to descend to reach the traverse, and it looked so hard that I thought it would require a fixed rope to ensure a safe retreat for the return of the tired summiteers. Its advantage was that, once across, we would be able to climb in one continuous push, without wasting more time on aid-climbing the rock or fixing more rope. Whatever happened, we both agreed that we would need at least three or four days of good weather. Our discussion about the route seemed academic as we sat in our sleeping bags with not the slightest let-up in the hurricane outside. We still clung to the hope that a dramatic change would come about, but our conversations were increasingly pessimistic.

A nagging concern was our lack of food. We had enough for two, possibly three days, and had expected to be supplied from Camp 1. We were like David Bowie's Major Tom – stuck for the time being beyond any hope of help. We casually idled the day away, shutting our minds to the banshee outside and the knowledge that, fit and healthy though we were, protected adequately in our Gortex bubble, we would soon be in a fatally serious situation if the wind did not moderate.

The second night, for me, was worse than the first. I had a foul headache, caused perhaps by cooking inside the tent. We had noticed that with the door zipped up the flame of the stove died down; there was not enough oxygen to feed it. Opening the door, however, allowed in a fine spray of ice particles as the wind whipped round the tent. Later, as I slipped into sleep, I entered a twilight zone of claustrophobia and nightmares, and so I struggled to stay awake, but as soon as I gave up the struggle the nightmares returned. My daytime lassitude was replaced by the suppressed fears of returning along the cornices – something that would have to be done eventually. All night I shivered and lay half-awake praying for the sun to restore some normality to my existence, and trying to think logically about my position.

From my diary, written a few days later

'Was I strong enough? Yes if the weather held fine. Was I as strong as the others? Probably not. Could be I'd be a hindrance, especially as we would be carrying big loads. Would the weather hold for the 3/4 days from Camp 2? I doubted it. The risk for me personally was beyond reasonable limits; it would not be fair on Mum, Dad and Lorna [my sister] to take such a risk. Better I pulled back and let stronger people do it, and helped them.

'Wouldn't people say I was scared? Yes, probably. Wasn't I missing the chance of a lifetime? Yes, undoubtedly. Missing also a chance to beat my Nun Kun altitude record of 23,410ft, and missing the view into Tibet. Missing doing the summit filming. But the final conclusion must be that it was way beyond my reasonable limits.

'My success was in putting the trip together.'

Shortly after dawn on 21 October I was aware that something had changed. I said to Jeff, 'Hey, Jackson, is it my overactive imagination or is the wind dropping?'

We listened. It was still howling but the note had changed. 'My boy, I think for once you might be right. Too early to say yet for sure, but could be we'll be out of here today.'

I told Jeff I had decided to move back to Camp 1 and give my place up to someone stronger, and that I would load-carry to Camp 2 in support of any summit party. Even then I still hung on to the hope that once the first group had completed the climb there might still be a chance for me. There was no emotion in our discussion, just talk of what was the most logical course to take. Jeff did not want to give up his pole position and preferred to leave his gear in the tent, come across to the snow dome with me, pick up some food and return to await – as he hoped – the arrival of Steve Monks.

An hour later the wind had dropped further and we decided to go. We took it in turns to don all our kit inside the tent before venturing outside, where the rucksacks were retrieved from between the snow bank and the back wall of the tent. I packed with my back to the wind and clipped on my crampons, setting off ahead of Jeff. The apprehension and stress of the danger to come made my movements on the first of the difficulties stiff and awkward, like a novice trying his first climb, but once I was past the friable cornice my confidence increased. The wind had veered further to the north, and gusted fitfully, trying with its remaining force to tear us from our precarious hold on the mountain. In a masochistic way I even found I enjoyed the fight with the rope and the wind. In two places the rope had bowed out and caught irretrievably round the cornices themselves. Swearing with fear, but with no alternative, I unclipped from the rope and climbed these sections relying on my two axes for safety. I told myself that the safety of the rope was purely in the mind anyway – not that it made me any the less frightened.

After three hours of constant fighting I reached the snow dome and sat there with my rucksack to the wind, waiting for Jeff. I dug into the dump for some nuts and raisins; all we had eaten at Camp 2 was soup, noodles, mash and fig-cakes. I sucked on the weighty lumps of ice hanging from my moustache and disciplined myself to wiggle my toes continuously to restore some life inside my double boots.

There was eventually a tap on my shoulder; Jeff, his beard also a mass of ice, looked haggard. His worried shouts in my ear came as no surprise: 'Steve, I really don't know whether I can make it back again.'

I had been sitting wondering whether this would happen when he got to me, but really he had little alternative; his sleeping bag and other personal gear were back in the tent.

'Well, Jeff,' I yelled back, 'you could come over to Camp 1 and borrow my duvet and bivi-bag to sleep in. There should be some room in the tents, provided Findlay and Lyd have not come back up . . .' I knew it was no use suggesting he go down to Advance Base Camp where there were spare pits – he would certainly lose his chance of a summit bid.

He kept glancing over his shoulder at the ridge, facing his decision. 'Shit, I'm going back. It's only taken us three hours to here – I'll make it.'

I stayed long enough to help him pack some food into his sack and then wished him good luck and left. Ten minutes later as I neared the Austrian tent the wind died even further. He would make it now, I thought.

As I arrived at Camp 1 at 12.30 p.m. I found Monksie and Ginette packing up their dome tent. With the drop in the wind they had decided to make a late dash across to Camp 2 taking their tent with them. As they hurried to leave they told me a confused story of how on 19 October they had heard over the radio from Harry, then at Base Camp, that the yaks had not been able to get through because the passes were too badly snowed up. Apparently it had taken Yeshey and Gopa five days through waist-deep snow drifts to reach Dur Sachu, and Harry had told them how four yak herders had eventually forced their way back up on foot through the Mangde Chu river gorge to Base Camp with meagre supplies and some mail. An even greater surprise was the news that there was talk of pulling us out by helicopter. If they had understood Harry correctly, they thought the Bhutanese staff would be leaving in five days time, except the radio operator Tobgay, and that we had been requested to clear the mountain. The last part I found hard to believe, as the expedition had paid for approximately sixty days in Bhutan and so far the main party had only been there forty-three days. In any case, we could not possibly leave yet; we were just coming to the crux of the climb. I was not going to call off our attempt on the basis of one garbled radio message.

Later in the afternoon Findlay and Lydia arrived carrying another dome tent, the Mars bars, some film for Al, and more food. Their version of the yaks story was slightly different. They knew nothing about a request for us to clear the mountain or the Bhutanese staff leaving.

They had heard of events via two letters carried by Phuntso, who had been sent up from Base Camp by Chris Lister with our first mail from England (most of the letters were dated mid-September) and some more food for Advance Base Camp. One letter was from

Yeshey, writing from Thimphu. It told us about the problem with the yaks, how he and Gopa had barely survived the five days to the hot springs, and how sorry he was that he could not rejoin us. He had returned to Thimphu and had recommended to his bosses that we be transported from the mountain by helicopter, as we would not be able to leave by yak. The other letter was from Chris Lister and said that there was some possibility of helicopter rescue, that he and Peter would be leaving in a few days, either with the kitchen staff down the river gorge or maybe by helicopter, and that Mark would probably stay to help with the final workload. I could sympathise with Chris wanting to leave: he and Mark had become forgotten members of the expedition and had now been at Base Camp with nothing to do for almost a month.

Phuntso's arrival with the letters was on 17 October, and Harry had tried that evening to contact us by radio but had received only Chinese-sounding voices and static. On 18 October Chris and Mark, who had not been to Advance Base Camp before, managed the journey to try and find out what the position was on the mountain. Chris had related to Harry the contents of his garbled radio conversation with the capital. He had received only an impression that Thimphu wanted us to evacuate the mountain. In the Tourism offices in the valley the officials had little idea of what conditions were like in the mountains; all they knew was that the passes had been closed by snow. They had expressed a strong concern to Chris about the onset of winter and the difficulties of evacuation. Chris's picture was vague. No definite plans had been made as yet and Harry therefore decided to return to Base to clarify the situation, taking with him the walkie-talkie so that he could relay information direct to the climbers.

It was some relief to know that Harry would be in control of the situation at Base Camp. He had the wherewithal and the right manner to handle a potentially delicate situation with the authorities. His career as a Royal Marines officer had left an indelible mark. He would be firm but fair and I knew that he could be trusted to do the right thing, though I worried that he would not remember the Bhutanese Mountaineering Rules and Regulations well enough to answer any questions about payment for the helicopters.

Findlay and Lydia also sprung the surprise that Al was half an hour behind them. Immediately I heard this I felt a thrill of pleasure. Al would know for himself now just exactly what it was like for us up on the mountain. When he arrived we shook hands and I gripped his shoulder.

'Al, you made it, you old bugger, you made it. It's really good to see you. Here, have a cup of soup. You must be absolutely knackered.' I laughed in real enjoyment at seeing him. 'I honestly never thought you'd make it up those ropes. Did you manage to do any filming? Hey, Al, have we got a treat in store for you tomorrow! You'll be able to film the 'dinosaur' from the top of the snow dome.'

He grinned back, extremely proud to have accomplished a climb harder than anything he had done before. 'Yeah, I never thought I would either. Did a bit of filming. God, I'm so tired, and I've got a splitting headache. I just want to lie down and die somewhere. We'll have to see about the snow dome. The way I feel right now I won't be going anywhere tomorrow.'

'Believe me, I know how you feel! What you need is plenty of liquids; you probably dehydrated badly today. Why don't you lie down for a bit? There's room for you in the dome with Steve and Lydia.'

The next day all four of us did in fact set off for the snow dome – Findlay and Lydia to stay at Camp 2 and join the summit bid, me to carry a load, and Al to do some filming. The weather was fine, with only a breeze on the lower part of the ridge. At the Austrian tent Al could not face the thought of another forward step. Although the wind was rising I knew that it was only another half-hour to the top of the snow dome and tried hard to persuade him to make one more effort, but he was content to leave the Scupic inside the half-buried wigwam, and return to Camp 1.

I followed on behind the other two, and with the second of the clockwork cameras I tried to film them crossing the 'dinosaur'. The wind was again so strong that removing mitts to operate the camera resulted in numbed hands within half a minute, and trying to change film cassettes and adjust the focus with the mitts on entailed the risk of dropping the cartridges or making mistakes. At the start the camera worked well, but by halfway it too had frozen up like the other one.

I confess to having felt very reluctant to re-cross the cornices, but I knew that the three ropes and the camera I was carrying were essentials for a summit attempt. I told myself that whatever happened I would turn back at 2.30 p.m. to allow time to reach Camp 1 by nightfall. Halfway along, a rare and most unusual thing happened – I saw the most perfect Brocken Spectre I've ever seen. The sun was behind me and cloud had formed on the southern side of the ridge where the pressure dropped as the wind passed over it. Suddenly I saw a circular rainbow against the cloud backdrop, with my shadow thrown into the centre of it. I could not remember whether this was supposed to be a good or a bad omen, but whichever it was I was held in wonder by this rare phenomenon of nature. I took a photograph but regrettably the shot turned out to be overexposed.

The total exhaustion of high-altitude climbing meant that I was taking longer and longer rests with fewer and fewer steps in between and by the time I did reach Camp 2 my body craved prolonged rest, but because it was now past three o'clock I felt like a man who had walked as far as he could tied to a large elastic band – one more step and the elastic band would pull him back to where he had started. I knew it would be dark in three hours. It was a long, long way back to my sleeping bag and there is no forgiveness in the mountains for those who overstep the mark; the wind might decide to resume its more natural inclination to be a hurricane and then I really would be in serious trouble. I felt like a burglar who can hear the police entering the front door as he tries to climb out of the back window. I desperately wanted to rest but was also frantic to leave.

I dumped the ropes and camera, proud of my effort, all the time talking, taking in the situation. The mood was full of optimism again. This was it! In two days they would go as a group to the summit; tomorrow Monksie and Jeff would fix the ropes across the traverse. They had obviously dropped the rock buttress idea. Wise decision, I had thought with relief.

I had obviously blown it; there was little chance that I could join in the attempt. It was too much to expect me to be able to do a repeat of today and still have enough energy for the summit. I listened to their plans, feeling excited that the attempt was on but crying inside that I was not going. The moments were too short, I had to go, and they knew I was saying goodbye to my chances. For me the work of two years, the strain and conflicts along the way, the dreams, the sacrifices ended there. Lydia tried to persuade me to come up again the next day, and I said I would think about it, knowing in my heart that it was over. She even took off her balaclava and goggles to kiss me goodbye. A nice gesture in freezing conditions. I agreed that whether I decided to come or not I would bring the small tent as far as the snow dome. If they wanted to take it with them one of them could fetch it on the day the traverse was being fixed.

I told them that I had not been able to get through to Harry on the walkie-talkie yet, but that in any event our budget would only stretch so far and they ought to aim to get down to Advance Base Camp on the 28th or 29th. In any case, no one was any longer concerned in the slightest with thoughts of leaving; nothing was more important than the last-ditch attempt. The third world war could have started and we would have taken no notice.

I registered dimly a story Monksie was telling me of how literally thirty yards from where we were standing, as he arrived at Camp 2, a cornice the size of a double-decker bus had broken away right next to him. The fracture line had passed within six inches of his right foot. A narrow escape.

Jeff's head stuck out of the tent and he looked at me with a worried or sad expression, I couldn't decide which. I reached in and shook Steve Findlay's hand. He smiled quietly at me. I was thinking of his wife, Angela, and his son, Ben. 'We'll do it for you, Steve,' he said. Ginette was in the back of the tent adding another smile to the emotional farewell. I felt morbid anxiety for their safety over the next few days; these were some of the best friends I had, and if the weather allowed they would be taking the final gamble, reliant only on their own resources if something should go wrong. On the other hand it seemed that with five fit people, now equipped with all that they needed, the chances of success were very high.

I wished them all luck and put all thoughts out of my mind, concentrating only on each placement of the axe, every kick of my cramponed feet, every pull on the jumar; fighting to stay relaxed, calm, to stave off the fear, to savour the thought of safety at the end of the 'dinosaur'. By the time I reached the snow dome I was chortling to myself. There was no hurry now. I knew I was safe.

I clipped into the rope and began the long descent. The sun was falling towards the western horizon, and the colours, so constant during the day, began their chemical-like change. First, at the edges of the world the sky began to bleach, almost white for a time, before hints of orange grew out of the horizon. The further I went the louder became the volume of change. The banks of colour widened, deepened, finally compelling me to hang on the rope to watch. To the west between all the peaks were fluffy balls of cotton wool, drifting slowly southwards, as in a tide. Beyond the tiny lake, where I knew our Base Camp to be, they massed over Bhutan, a sea of soft innocuous-looking material, beautiful but potentially lethal. The horizon became a broad belt of violent orange topped with subtler hints of vermilion and pink. Beneath me I watched cloud forming and billowing south from a ridge two thousand feet below; it was as though the ridge was burning and the clouds were its yellow smoke. Kanchenjunga and Chomolhari were islands of peach in the darkening horizon. As the sun came closer and closer to its final blaze the white of the land grew darker, turning pastel purple.

I was cold but have rarely felt happier. I felt privileged and offered words of thanks and incredulity to the maker I do not believe in. More than that, I felt a sense of timelessness, humble that my life and the things in it counted for nothing compared with the vast and wonderful world in front of me. I sang as I came down the ropes, and from 250 feet above Camp 1 could dimly make out Al shovelling snow from around the tent. I yelled, hoping to share my joy with another person, but he couldn't hear.

I lay inside my sleeping bag as Al prepared supper, relishing the comfort of muscles no longer straining at every step. By the time I remembered, we had missed the 7 p.m. radio call; I hoped Harry would not think our set was broken and give up trying us every night. We talked for a long time after we had finished eating, and continued after we had turned our head torches off, about our respective families, until my eyes closed of their own accord and Al received snores instead of replies.

At 11.30 p.m. I was woken by the sounds of another gale battering our tent, and I lay awake for hours listening to the wind and struggling to decide whether to go back to Camp 2 to join the summit bid. I kept telling myself that this would be my last chance. What I think I feared was that with my strength dwindling I could have become stuck by a storm near the summit and died through weakness, as Al Rouse had done earlier in the year on K2. Norman

Croucher, the disabled climber, had made the decision I was now making on our expedition to Nun Kun in 1981 and we had all respected him for it. He had decided that by continuing he was jeopardising the chances of two other people reaching the summit, and had unselfishly waited at the bivouac for their return. Was it fear or was it unreasonable for me to continue? The questions and answers repeated themselves *ad nauseam* with no satisfactory conclusion.

The dawn of 23 October brought no let-up in the wind. Only briefly after lunch was there a lull, allowing us to move around outside. We mended a broken tent pole and re-anchored the dome with our four ice axes, the two snow shovels, a couple of dead men and some ski sticks.

At 6 p.m. we finally managed to raise Harry on the walkie-talkie. His familiar voice came faintly through the static from Base Camp. Al and I strained to pick up the gist of each sentence, as slowly and deliberately Harry repeated his messages. We were to be helicoptered out by an Indian Army helicopter. He told us that he needed to give Thimphu five days notice. When did we want the chopper? He had provisionally said to them 30 October. What did I think? I asked him to call again in five minutes while I thought about it.

Al and I imagined the sequence of possible events:

24 October SM and JJ fix the traverse.
25–27 October To the summit and return to Camp 2.
28 October Return to Advance Base Camp.
29 October Resting and packing loads.
30 October Drag everything across the glacier, dump most of it at
            the start of the moraine crossing, sleep at Base Camp.
31 October
to   Ferry loads from dump on glacier to Base Camp.
2 November
3 November Begin evacuation of Base Camp by helicopter.

This still left enough leeway for an extra day or two on the mountain but the climbers would have to leave Camp 2 for the top by 26 October at the latest.

Harry came on the air and I told him 3 November for the helicopters. He then told me that Pete, Chris and Mark were to be helicoptered out the following day and that Pete was hoping to try and take the film gear out by truck through Assam. There was something about supplies being dropped by helicopter but we couldn't make out whether it had already happened or whether it was expected. Finally I asked Harry whether there had been any mention of who was going to pay for all this and he replied no.

24 October dawned and still the wind blew hard. Al and I had now been in the tent for a day and two nights. We were both determined to go up the ridge whatever the conditions – Al to do his filming, but mainly because I had promised to take the small tent as far as the snow dome. At 10 a.m. we packed the rucksacks, put on every article of clothing and left the tent.

It was one thing making vows inside a tent but quite another performing them when faced with a wind that took the breath from our lungs and blasted our faces with fine particles of ice. We pretended to ignore the inevitable decision by strapping on crampons, digging out our ice axes, shouldering our rucksacks. It was a farce. We stood outside the tent pulling on our goggles, standing with our backs to the wind, and looked at each other.

Al shouted, 'This is crazy, isn't it?'

'Yeah, this is crazy all right,' I laughed into the wind.

'We can't go up there in this, can we?'

'No, I don't suppose so.'

So saying, without taking one step past the tent, we returned to our sleeping bags, to continue the round of brews, cards and talking.

I was fascinated to know how Al had become a film director living in Leeds from being a kid in the East End of London. His father had owned a scaffolding business and when Al was only a young boy his uncle had been killed in a scaffolding accident. His father had refused to allow Al to come into the firm and he had found a job as a 'runner' at Shepperton Studios. He was promoted to tea boy and once inside the building he had picked up the skills of a film editor by assisting wherever he could. Gradually he had become involved in editing important programmes and feature films. The work had taken him to Yorkshire TV, and it was during this time that he was approached by Chris Bonington to make a film about the 1978 expedition to K2, the world's second highest mountain. Yorkshire TV had not been keen on the project and so

Al had set up his own firm to produce the film. Since then his company, Chameleon Films, had become specialists in directing and producing adventure documentaries, particularly mountaineering films. Al himself had been on a number of these expeditions, including Everest in winter with Al Rouse, and K2 in 1978, and as a result had become close friends with many of the famous British mountaineers – Chris Bonington, Don Whillans, Joe Tasker, Pete Boardman – most of whom had died in the intervening years. It was a standing joke that Al's personal equipment was made up of bits and pieces of dead men's gear.

It seems to me that Al is one of those people who have an almost endless supply of energy. He has several projects in the air at any one time, not all of them films necessarily. He also owns a travel company and a recording company, and he juggles all these projects until some fall to the ground and others come to fruition. He is a very likeable man, living in a highly competitive profession, doing his best to be honest in situations which, the film industry being what it is, seemed highly complicated to me.

I had just finished listening with fascination to a much more extended version of his life story – including chapters about a wilder, less responsible man than he was that day – when we both were shocked to hear a female voice outside the tent.

16
Wrecked Tent

We looked at each other registering the same thought; had something tragic occurred? It was Lydia. She banged the snow off her clothes, crawled in and flopped on to the mound of down sleeping bags.

'It's no good. We decided to call it off. The wind's horrendous. Yesterday Monksie and Jeff tried to do the traverse but it took them four hours just to go four hundred feet. They've both got frost nip in their fingers and toes. It's just so fucking cold up there. They only got about a third of the way across and they said the ice was too hard to get your axe into. Desperate. Just no way, Steve. No way.' Her eyes held none of their almost permanent sparkle. They looked at her feet, glanced at me occasionally. She was probably wondering what my reaction to their decision would be.

It did not really surprise me, and the depression at our failure did not sink in until much later. Right there and then I was just happy to see that they were safe. One by one they arrived, looking terribly tired, Jeff, late starting as usual, bringing up the rear with Ginette, who was suffering from stomach trouble.

There was unanimous and total conviction that an attempt on the summit had been quite impossible. The feeling was more that in the circumstances they were lucky to have got back across the corniced ridge at all. The fact was that the winter winds had arrived much earlier than expected. We had arrived at Base Camp almost exactly at the end of the monsoon, but the usual spell of settled weather between the monsoon and winter had simply not materialised.

The atmosphere was one of disbelief at the constant ferocity of the wind and the extreme cold, and happy relief that the climb was over. We even laughed, taking enjoyment from the fact that soon we would be drinking beer back in Thimphu. Jeff showed me the whitened ends of his fingertips; they would recover, but he would probably lose feeling in them for a month or two, and the dead skin would peel off and be replaced.

They all decided to carry on after a rest to reach **Advance Base Camp** that night, but since Al wanted to recover the Scupic from where it had been left in the Austrian tent I decided to stay with him one more night. He still wanted to reach the snow dome to obtain good-quality film of the 'dinosaur'.

After two more abortive attempts at radio contact with Harry in the evening, we settled down for the night at 8 p.m. I had slept so badly for the last week that I almost took a sleeping pill. I don't like taking them as they have the effect of depressing one's breathing rate, which can be dangerous at altitude. It is a good thing I decided not to.

At 3 a.m. I woke and knew immediately that something was wrong. Al was sitting up pushing against the wall of the tent to prevent it collapsing completely. The wind had risen to a level of ferocity we had not experienced there at Camp 1 before. The immediate threat was that the tent, unless supported, would split open.

'I think part of the fly has come off,' he yelled.

'OK, Al, we'll have to get the rucksacks and the Kariamats and sit with our backs to the wall.'

Hurriedly we piled everything we could behind us and, still inside our sleeping bags, braced ourselves against the inner skin, as the wind, now perhaps 70–80 m.p.h., lashed at the fabric. It shook us like dolls as we fought to stop it doubling us over. Part of the fly had indeed come loose and whipped at our backs. We could not tell how long it would be before the tent would split open but we knew that if it did survival might not be possible. Would the anchors hold? Would we find ourselves blown right off the mountain? What if this lasted for thirty-six hours, as it had done at Camp 2?

Every few minutes we turned on our head torches and examined the fabric for signs of tearing. We gathered together all the essentials for our survival, putting on all our gloves, our balaclavas, and last, with the greatest of difficulty, even our boots.

Slowly the tent disintegrated around us. The poles either broke or disappeared altogether. At one point I received a heavy blow on the leg – an axe anchor had come out and was flying about like a thing possessed. I managed to grab it as it hurtled into the fabric again and again, and found that I could barely stop it from being wrenched out of my grasp, even though I was holding it with two hands.

I shouted in Al's ear, 'Al, for Christ's sake, get the penknife out of the top pocket of my rucksack, unzip the door and I'll try and drag it in so you can cut it free.'

The axe was wound up in a tangle of guy lines and parts of the fly. Having pulled it inside, after a prolonged fight, I held it with both hands and tried to keep it steady. The fact that we were being battered around ourselves meant that cutting the axe free was going to be a hazardous exercise. We bent over it, trying to illuminate the problem with our fading head torches. Al sawed successfully through the messed knot of nylon line and fly sheet, managing by luck not to sever my fingers, and zipped up the door again.

We were frightened that the snapped poles would pierce the skin of the tent and start a major tear, but although both the inner and outer were now full of holes the fabric stubbornly refused to rip. Thank God for rip-stop nylon.

The whole of our world was a crazy, jumping, banging, frenzied, noisy bag of nylon, but even so there was one peaceful presence – the moon. She shone dimly through the roof of thrashing fabric, uncaring of our plight, a subtle, incongruous spectator. The only physical stillness in our world of deafening noise and manic anger was the sleeping bags which we were hunched up in.

We were obviously both scared by the sheer power of nature's forces which at any second might obliterate our insignificant little shelter, but no panic entered our actions. At the time it had seemed that we were not far removed from death, and perhaps because of this our teamwork was near-perfect. There was an almost telepathic sense of knowing exactly what had to be done. A minimum of words were spoken and for the next six or seven hours we withstood the constant buffeting with enforced patience and watchfulness. Towards dawn I had become so tired and dazed from sitting upright that I could no longer maintain my alertness and dozed fitfully. Dawn gave us back our sight, gave us hope that we would be able to escape. We were by now both bursting to go to the loo and we took it in turns, with extreme difficulty, to kneel and piss into an Austrian orange-powder container. Opening the door, I flung it outside, glimpsing breathtaking sunrise colours. I would have loved to take a photograph but, with the wind still howling, there was no way I was going to put my head out of the door.

The hours passed by and the storm began to moderate. By mid-morning there were ten- or twenty-second breaks when the wind halved in strength. We formed a huddle in the middle of our wrecked, wildly flapping, expensive dome tent, and by holding on to the stove and the billy we managed to melt some ice for some muesli and coffee. There was no question but that the Scupic camera, with valuable exposed film inside, would have to be abandoned. The only thought on our minds was escape.

At 10.30 a.m. we had packed and emerged into the open. We had to lean into the wind, covering our faces with our arms. We abandoned the tent to its fate. It was now like a tethered balloon, held by two guys whose pegs were frozen into the ice. I thought that it would not be long before it flew into the air like a bird.

I was worried for Al. He had done comparatively little abseiling and at each rope change-over he fumbled with his descendeur. His actions did not have the automatic fluency of repeated practice. My major worry was that he would make a mistake in the vertical rock sections before reaching the Japanese gully. I sent him down first, checking his gear and repeating instructions to him on how to make himself safe at the belays. With two of us to pull on the ropes we were just able to thread his descendeur where previously I had used only a twist in my harness-caribiner to slide down the rope.

I remember a time rock climbing in the Verdon Gorge in France, where, 1,250ft up a limestone cliff, a friend and I had been forced to retreat in a snowstorm by abseil, and on that occasion practically everything that could go wrong went wrong. Ropes had stuck, abseil devices had been dropped, head torches had failed and we had arrived at the base of the cliff sodden and frozen. We had tried to be careful, but in difficult circumstances things have a habit of going wrong. However, for Al and me the descent went perfectly, except that Al was hit on the shoulder by a falling rock at the bottom of the ramp. He was not hurt badly, though from his hesitant speech I wondered whether he was concussed at all. We stumbled on, desperately tired now from lack of sleep and food. One hundred yards from camp a crampon came off and trailed behind me, its strap still tied to my ankle. We must have looked a pathetic sight as we arrived.

'Has anyone got a brew? You'll never believe what a night we had last night. The tent blew down,' I said.

'Yeah? That sounds bad. It was pretty windy here too. Did you recover the tent?' Steve Findlay replied.

'No, it wasn't worth it. The thing was a wreck, and anyway it was too windy to hang around.'

Our night of intense struggle was already an incident in the past, and only Al and I would ever know what it had really been like. Right then we had to address ourselves to the more urgent issues of helicopters and evacuation.

The next day dawned sunny and calm at Advance Base Camp. Was the mountain laughing at us now she had thrown us off? Were the others hasty in leaving? Should they have stayed another day? Was it actually as still up there as it looked?

Harry had come up from Base to help strip Advance Base Camp and he told us that he and the Bhutanese staff sitting at Base had wondered what we were making a fuss about: down there it had been clear sunny skies and hardly a breath of wind. To them it seemed that the weather was perfect for climbing; our reports on the radio of gales and hurricanes had seemed strange.

We knew in our hearts that it was still blowing across the ridge just as strongly as ever; we could in fact see the long streamers of snow feathering the summit, silhouetted against the blue of the sky.

In any event, there was no time to stew in failure; we needed to dismantle the tents and pack everything into our rucksacks. What we could not carry, four of us would drag across the glacier in two of the huge red haul bags that had originally brought the expedition equipment from England. The other two Steves and Lydia had by this time already departed for Base carrying enormous rucksacks.

Since arriving at the mountain our Bhutanese friends had asked us not to burn rubbish. We had expected this, as the same had happened in Nepal; it is a Buddhist belief that each of the large mountains is itself a god and that the god should not be angered by the burning of refuse in its presence. However, now that we were departing burning the rubbish was a necessity; the god could be as angry as he or she liked. We also left a dump of food and equipment that we no longer needed for whoever was to come next to court Gangkar Punsum. This included my old petrol stove. I was sad to see it go, it had been on many adventures, but, as Lydia had pointed out in one of our early conversations, there is no good in living in the past by clinging to sentimental attachments. I could see her point, though I did not agree with it entirely.

When the time to set off finally came I felt that same sadness one has when parting from a friend knowing that one will not see him again for a long time. I did not want to leave, and here at Advance Base Camp we were close to the mountain, holding on to her still. Soon we would be at Base, at the doorway, waving; it would not be the same. After so long living with Gangkar Punsum she had in my mind taken on a personality; although the logic of a Western upbringing refuted it utterly, I could not help thinking of her sometimes as an all-knowing, all-seeing entity. This ridiculous concept was never voiced openly but occasionally I picked up hints that I was not alone in my love for her – not merely as a piece of beautiful snow and rock but also as a force that had affected our lives in a powerful and equally beautiful way.

We attached a rope with loops to the two haul bags and like a team of huskies we pulled away across the glacier, singing a loud chorus of 'Rawhide'. It was yet another exhausting day, enlivened by riding one of the big red bags down a long snow slope, and spoilt by my letting rip at Jeff for no good reason, a silly outburst of bad temper. Dreams are not the only way of flushing repressed tensions, and maybe I needed to have a good shout at somebody. Jeff was the unfortunate recipient, but afterwards I knew I had made a fool of myself and apologised.

At the junction with the main glacier we dumped the haul bags for collection the following day and began the laborious journey through the chaotic jumble of the moraine. As on every crossing, I fell behind the others and as usual Harry was waiting for me on the other side.

'Hi, Harry. Thought you'd be here. Thanks for waiting.'

'That's OK, mate. You feeling all right?'

'Yeah, I guess so.'

'Have five minutes, then. Not far now. Another half-hour and you'll be drinking Phuntso's excuse for tea.'

We arrived after dark to a warm welcome, all the kitchen staff, Tobgay and Gopa included, shaking us by the hand. I recall dropping my rucksack to the ground and thinking, 'One more trip across the moraine and that'll be the last time I have to lift that again this trip.'

17
Indian Helicopters

The news in camp was encouraging. Already Pete, Chris and Mark had been air-lifted out, and the helicopter had been rearranged for 29 October. There had even been some talk of two choppers to speed the operation up. Pleasure was in the fact that Gopa was unexpectedly there to greet us. I had imagined that he was in Thimphu with Yeshey after their ordeal crossing the passes. He diffidently described how they had slept under rocks on the snow-covered hillsides, and of becoming lost because the path had been covered in snow, before finally reaching the hot springs. He had then conscientiously returned with four of the yak men up the Mangde Chu river gorge, although there was no path of any sort, with the badly needed supplies and our mail.

Outwardly we were a happy crowd looking forward to a well deserved rest. We lusted for the good food and beer in Thimphu, hot baths, clean clothes and souvenir hunting. We all wanted nothing more than to indulge in lazy pastimes, listen to music and not to have to lift a finger to do anything. It is true that we entertained no doubts about how we had tackled the climb; there had been no major differences or rows. We had had five strong and fit climbers at the top camp with all the food and equipment necessary for a summit bid. We had pulled together as a team and we all knew that it was the weather and nothing else that had thwarted our ambitions. In this knowledge we suffered no guilt, there were no recriminations to be made, but the fact still remained that we had failed. Whether it was an underlying depression because of this or whether we had spent too long in each other's company I cannot say, but the fact is that petty bickering marred the remaining days at Base Camp.

On the morning of 27 October we gathered at breakfast and a discussion took place regarding fetching the loads that had been left on the other side of the glacier. We had all agreed before leaving Advance Base Camp that one carry by the whole team and some of the Bhutanese would complete the irksome task, but now Lydia complained of a cold and Monks declined to take part.

'Look, this is silly,' he said. 'It's just not necessary for us all to go across. There surely can't be more than eighty kilos over there – five or six loads at the most. You'll have Phuntso and Dorji; maybe you could persuade Gopa and Guncho to go as well. I say those of us that want to go, go. I for one don't.'

I wondered whether he was right. Was it only eighty kilos? Yesterday I had it in my mind that there were nine loads.

'Steve, we all agreed that we would all go back across the glacier and in any case I don't think you are right about the loads. I'm sure there's more than six. I also doubt that Gopa would do this kind of work – he's higher status than the rest.'

'Well, why don't you ask him?'

'I will do,' I retorted, on the defensive, 'but I still say it's unfair that just because you don't want to do it you should leave it to the rest of us. Jesus, I don't want to go, but that's not the point.'

My arguments sounded weak to my own ears; besides, everyone else was willing to do the carry. I backed off. He was certainly right, we did not all need to go, but a unilateral decision on his part was no way of deciding who was to go and who not. I felt angry and saddened by his attitude. I felt it was not the Steve Monks I had known in earlier days. I could remember times when he had shamed me for not being completely impartial, and had changed my position on an issue by his tactful, thoughtful manner. Perhaps his fame from having solo'd the Eiger and becoming the best rock climber in Australia had gone to his head, I thought. I decided he was lazy and told him so.

Four of the Bhutanese agreed to help with the load carrying, including Gopa, who would not hear of any payment, making eight of us altogether (Steve Findlay turned back halfway as he had forgotten his snow goggles). There were indeed nine loads, making the work much harder than it need have been, and, to inflame my indignation further, we found on arrival at the glacier dump that amongst the equipment were a large number of personal items belonging to those who had stayed in camp.

Nothing was said when we arrived back at Base but at the evening meal an opportunity to vent my feelings presented itself. Discussion had turned to who should take the first ride out in the helicopter.

I said, 'From what Tobgay tells me, if they do bring two choppers tomorrow then there will probably be room for at least three people, plus room for some gear. I think that those places should go to Al, Findlay and Harry.'

As usual there were a few wisecracks and some good-humoured laughter, but then Monksie chipped in with: 'What makes them so special that you think they should go first, Steve? Why not some of the rest of us instead?'

His wide grin and mock-serious tones indicated perhaps only a light-hearted attempt at frivolity, but in the mood I was in I saw in it an attempt to get himself back to the capital first.

In even tones I replied, 'Well, actually, the reasons I had in mind were that Al wants to get on and do some more filming in Thimphu, and wants Findlay to be in some of the shots, and I thought Harry ought to go as he has had to do all the work down here organising the choppers.' And then I added cuttingly, 'In any case, Steve, how can you leave your personal gear on the other side of the glacier, get other people to pick it up, and then expect to get the first ride out on the helicopter?'

It was not a question; it required no answer. The answer was in the catcalls and general murmur of approval. We have known each other too long and shared some of the best adventures of our lives for one row to affect a lifelong friendship, but at that moment the tension between us was real enough.

Had we placed just one person on the summit of Gangkar Punsum we would all have been living the days in constant celebration, and I am convinced that none of these tensions would have materialised. The achievement would have been something that we would have been proud of for the rest of our lives. As it was, we should have been satisfied with the fact that we came out of it alive and with some unforgettable, if not always pleasurable, experiences. Unfortunately, the human spirit is rarely satisfied with the good things it has got when it imagines that there are better things within reach. On reflection, perhaps I should have expected dissatisfaction to show itself amongst the seven of us after our failure, but the façade of everyone enjoying sunshine and music seemed real. I was unprepared for the rows that followed.

On 28 October the helicopters did not fly in. I went through the day in a melancholy mood, feeling separated from the others. It seemed to me that it was like being at a railway station. Many of the others were sitting in a waiting room impatient for the train to arrive, their surroundings already forgotten, whilst I stood on the platform clinging to something I was very unwilling to part from.

The radio generator and Tobgay's voice calling Thimphu at regular intervals throughout the day provided me with background interest. Listening in on some of the exchanges it seemed to me that our Bhutanese hosts in the capital could not cut through the Indian Army bureaucracy. Karchung Wangchuck was obviously trying his hardest but he could not establish the identity of the person who made the actual decision whether the helicopters would fly or not. In the amusing but frustrating way that the East in general has, no matter how concise the question put to the Indian army the answer would always be evasive, ambiguous or noncommittal. The decision would filter back to Thimphu through a complicated and untraceable chain of army and diplomatic personnel who seemed to be scattered across half India.

I was up at 5.30 a.m. on 29 October, anxious not to miss the last opportunity – as I thought – of seeing sunrise touch the mountains. I moved quietly through the still sleeping camp, dressed in my warmest down clothing against the subzero temperatures. The hard frost sparkled in the light of my head torch as I walked up to the small lake five minutes from camp. Independently, Steve Findlay and Jeff had had the same thought, and we waited, shivering, as the eastern horizon started to dress itself for another day. I felt reassured that I was not the only one who was sorry to be leaving. Dawn amazed us again with its subtle light show. I remember particularly the whispy clouds which appeared to be tethered above the 'sacred' lake, and how they had turned gentle pink for just a few minutes before dissolving under the heat of the sun.

As the shadows moved out of camp, people began to stir. Smoke rose from Phuntso's fire. We could hear him muttering his morning prayers and shouting at lazy Dorji, still sleeping in the mess tent. The generator started, charging the radio battery for another round of garbled conversation with our friends eighty miles away in Thimphu.

At 10 a.m. we heard with excitement that two helicopters had arrived from India and were already on their way to pick us up. Apparently the flight would take about an hour. We waited, straining our ears for the first sounds, but nothing came. On the midday radio call we were told that the pilots had been unable to find us and had turned back.

During the morning a further row had broken out between myself and Monks. I had asked that if anyone wanted to give presents for the kitchen staff they should leave the gifts outside my tent. The only two people not to give anything were Monksie and Lydia. I was incensed. Yet another show of selfishness, I thought. In the most sarcastic tones I could summon I said to Monks, 'Hey, Steve, why don't you give them your camera? It's not working anyway, so you won't need it any more.'

I could hardly have said anything more insulting, but his reply stung back.

'Look, Steve, if I don't want to give a present then that's my decision. I'm not going to be told to do it just because you think it's a nice idea.'

I stomped off. In a way I could not fault his reasoning: if he didn't want to give a present then I had no right to force him to. I wondered whether he was merely reacting to too autocratic an attitude on my part. Misuse of authority was something I had always held in contempt myself. Nevertheless, I felt he and Lydia were being particularly mean after all the hard work and friendship Phuntso and the others had given us.

Around midday two Ravens circled camp and Harry pronounced that it was a sure sign that the pilots would find us. He was right. At 2.15 p.m. the drone of engines could be heard to the south. Phuntso, whooping with delight, raced down to the level landing area we had marked out near the lake to light a fire. Two machines appeared over the ridge to the south. As they came in to land, shattering the peace of the last five weeks, there was a general rush for the landing area. I stayed by the kitchen, filming the take-off at Al's request, and saw four people climb up into the two perspex cockpits. The deafening noise increased and the two machines rose twenty feet off the ground, hovered, and then landed again. One person jumped out of each helicopter, ducked and ran under the whirling blades to the edge of the field as the pilots finally rose to a hundred feet, turned, and raced off southwards.

It was Harry who walked over to me and said, 'I'll give you three guesses who left in the helicopters, Steve. No, don't bother to guess, I'll tell you. It was Monksie and Lydia!'

Again the hated emotions of disgust and anger welled up inside
me. All the effort we had all been to over the past few weeks and the
last two years, and it had to be spoilt by such selfish behaviour. The
very fact that we were in one of the most beautiful places on God's
earth did not alter the fact that we as human beings could not
behave decently to each other. Universal condemnation followed
their departure and it was with some mirth that we all heard on the
radio that they had been dropped at Bumthang and that the
helicopters were coming back to pick more of us up; we would be
taken to Thimphu and Monksie and Lydia would have to travel by
lorry to meet us later. We were to be disappointed, however, as on
returning the helicopter pilots decided the cloud in the Mangde
Chu valley had become too thick. They abandoned the second
pick-up, collected Monks and Lydia and dropped them off in Paro.

Monksie came through on the radio two days later, acutely
embarrassed at their mistake. He explained that he and Lydia had
just piled in with everyone else, expecting that six people would be
lifted that afternoon, as there were three empty seats in the back of
each aircraft, and not thinking that they would be the ones to be
given the first flights. Within minutes we had re-established the
familiar bonds of friendship as though nothing had happened.
However, the afternoon they had departed marked a low point in
the expedition – failure on the mountain, followed by a breakdown
of the clean atmosphere of friendship that we had started our
adventure with.

The helicopter evacuation, having started on time with two
machines, seemed certain to be complete within a matter of days.
On the following day just one aircraft arrived, but it made two
flights and carried two climbers on each occasion and only Ginette
and I and the four Bhutanese were left behind.

It was at this point that the Indian army seemed to lose a sense
of urgency regarding our evacuation. During the next eight days
there were seven abortive attempts to reach us at Base. Also,
because there was an important religious festival that the pilots
wanted to attend in India, for three days there were no flights at all.
If there was an Indian officer planning the operation he made a
number of elementary mistakes. Having discovered that it was
difficult to locate us without maps of the region, instead of the
pilots who had learnt how to find Base Camp new aircrews were

used on subsequent flights who had no idea how to find us. One imagined that from the air the highest mountain in the kingdom would be easy to spot, but apparently it was not.

As the days passed slowly by we became more and more frustrated at the inability of the Indian bureaucrats to act upon the simple instructions we attempted to relay to them. The key to the problem was making the flight early in the morning. By midday the approach route up the Mangde Chu river gorge always filled with cloud, formed by Gangkar Punsum. However, instead of staying overnight at the helipad at Tongsa, twenty minutes flying time from Base Camp, or even at Paro, the pilots insisted on returning each day to Hashimare in India. Consequently their late arrival at Paro became as predictable as the meals of rice and lentils that were all that Phuntso now had left in his kitchen.

From my diary – 6 November

'Crazy day. It was going to be early chopper or walk-out. Practically all the food gone. Perfect weather, hopes are sky high. 7 a.m. radio call and since then every half-hour. It is 3 p.m. and we're still here.

'The problem is that one has to first speak with the Paro radio operator, who then telephones the airport officer, who contacts the Indian army – or Karchung has to be located. Misinformation is the result; nobody ever seems to be able to give precise information.

'The pilots did not stay overnight in Paro, and first off we're told they left India at 6.40 a.m. and were coming straight here – 1½ hours, we reckon. We sit and watch and strain our ears, the minutes pass, what can have happened? Bad weather in India? Technical problems? Ran out of fuel? Crashed? Stopped in Paro?

'Later, after several abortive radio attempts, we find out they haven't left at all; they were only *expected* to leave at 6.40 a.m. Are they coming? No one knows. Karchung, who spoke to us at 7 a.m., cannot be found. We tell the radio operator that we must know by 10.30 a.m. what is happening or we are walking out.

'Asked at 10.30 a.m. to wait till 11 a.m. Very fed up by now and reluctant to wait. Gopa wants Thimphu's permission before leaving. We wait. At 11 a.m. we're told the thing has left India.

'At 12.30 a.m. it has not come. They tell us ETA is 12.50 a.m. We all sit and watch the valley. 1.10 p.m. We had given up hope when we heard it coming. Frantic joy. All our cursing Indians and kicking stones angrily gave way to a rush for the rucksacks, and Phutso going apeshit lighting the fire.

'*But* the sounds recede. Of course it had been perfectly clear all morning, but at 12.45 a.m. cloud had started to appear in the gorge.

'Surely they could make it through, it wasn't that bad, but no, we wait and wait. Nothing!

'I'm very angry. Stupid – – Indians; they ought to be driving rickshaws in Delhi, not flying helicopters.

'A whole day wasted. If only they had come early we would be out. Who knows what the weather will be like tomorrow.

'Find out at 3 p.m. that they had just got lost! How crazy can you get?

'Pilots come to the radio at 3.30 p.m. and I describe how to get to Base Camp, urge them to stay overnight in Bhutan and come between 6 and 7 a.m. for good weather. They agree.'

Later that afternoon something remarkable happened. I spotted an eagle in the sky, soaring in circles above the ridge between us and Gangkar Punsum. Within half an hour more had arrived, and whilst walking up on to the top of the ridge I spotted no less than twenty-eight. Some of them were so high I could barely make them out, but others circled two hundred feet above me. They had black tips on their wings and one was completely white – probably a young one, I decided. I sat watching them for an hour as they soared above the ridge. As the sun bloodied the sky in the west and the freezing temperatures forced me back to camp, my last memory was of them silhouetted, circling a rocky peak over towards Lunana. What had brought them to this place, where were they going, and where had they come from? Gopa thought they came from Lhasa in Tibet, but I think he was only guessing. Even Dasho Penjor Darji, the expert on the black-necked cranes, was puzzled when I met him again in Thimphu.

The next morning we were told that the helicopter had left Paro at 6.50 a.m. Gopa, Tobgay and I placed bets on the time of arrival. By 8.15 we had all given up hope when the faint noise of its motor was heard and we spotted a small speck in the sky. It was so small that it had to be at an altitude of 19,000 or 20,000ft. Convinced that even the Indians could not fail now, we rushed down to the landing area and lit the fires. The machine disappeared round the other side of Gangkar Punsum and did not reappear. The very last shreds of faith in the Indian army evaporated, and we made an irrevocable decision to leave. The tents were collapsed and the rubbish burnt with the last of the generator's petrol. The radio crackled and an almost hysterical Karchung pleaded with us to wait one more time, saying that the helicopter would have Yeshey on board to show the pilots the way. We refused. We had decided that as there was now only a bare minimum of food left we had to leave. Karchung pleaded again, saying that the helicopter was definitely on its way, that Yeshey was at the helipad at Thimphu waiting to be picked up. We pointed out to him the difficulties of the river gorge with no footpath, insisting that it was imperative that we leave at the latest by 11 a.m. No, he said, we must wait until 12 to allow for the helicopter to turn round. We waited. Noon came and went, and the radio was by this time alive with reports on the helicopter's progress. After so many abortive flights even the almost inexhaustible patience of the Bhutanese had disappeared and they were as angry as we were. No one could believe that something would not go wrong. At 12.45 p.m. it had still not arrived and just as we were hefting our sacks to begin the seven- or eight-day walk-out it flew over the ridge from the south-west.

As it touched down we all danced on the edge of the field, shaking hands and laughing our goodbyes. No more rice and lentils, no more freezing nights, no more hours by the radio with Gopa and Tobgay, no more evenings round Phuntso's fire listening to his songs, and goodbye to the watchful presence of Gangkar Punsum. The two Indian pilots sat nodding their heads in the way all Indians do, smiling and sucking on a tube that they passed to each other – oxygen for the altitude, I thought. The noise was deafening. Yeshey emerged and ran, ducking, towards us. There was no time to stop and talk. Ginette and I just stumbled over the rough ground, carrying three rucksacks and a tent between us. We squeezed into the rear seat, the rucksacks on our laps. The noise increased, we heard the pilots doing their final checks, we started to lift. The engines seemed to be working at full capacity and yet we were only just lifting off. We sank down again. 'Oh, no,' I thought, 'they'll ask us to dump the rucksacks.' Instead, the senior pilot half-opened his door and waved to Yeshey. Ginette and I exchanged incredulous glances – they were going to take another!

For all the frantic rush of events and excitement at the thought of flying over Bhutan, there still remained a quietness inside myself. As we finally rose higher above Base Camp, Phuntso and the others still waving, figures in a silent movie, I turned to look at the mountain again. Living with her had been so intense that my own future had been forgotten. Now the practical complications of life were rushing towards me again and her beauty was perhaps a closed chapter in my life.

Appendix
Expedition Members

Climbing Members

Steven Berry (Leader) Age 37, single. Five Himalayan climbing expeditions, including in 1981 the first British ascent of Nun Kun, 23,410ft, the highest peak in Indian Kashmir, attempted by his father in 1946. The 1981 expedition included amongst its members Norman Croucher, the disabled climber, who achieved a record altitude for a disabled climber of 22,000ft. The author's other interests include caving, subaqua diving and hang-gliding. He is now a co-director in a company specialising in trekking holidays to the Himalaya.

Lydia Bradey Age 24, single. Four Himalayan expeditions to her credit, including an ascent of the world's thirteenth highest mountain, Gasherbrum II, 26,355ft, in the Karakoram. She is a New Zealander who can also claim to be one of the world's best women 'big wall' climbers, having made many ascents of the hardest multi-day rock climbs in America. She is completely committed to climbing, which for her is now a full-time occupation.

Stephen Findlay (Food Officer) Age 31, married. At present Steve teaches at a special school for disadvantaged children. His one previous Himalayan expeditiion was to Cho Oyu, 26,906ft, the world's sixth highest mountain. All the expedition members, bar Ginette Harrison, took part in that expedition, which also included Dr Norman Waterhouse, a mountaineer well known for his research into the physical effects of high-altitude climbing. Steve's special interest is botany, and Bhutan's relatively unknown flora was to be for him an added bonus.

Dr Ginette Harrison (Medical Officer) Age 28, single. Also well known for her high-altitude medical research, Ginette's expeditions include climbs in Nepal, Pakistan, Alaska and Africa. After the expedition she spent a period of time working in a small hospital close to Annapurna, where she treated not only climbers and trekkers but the local people as well.

Jeff Jackson (Co-Medical Officer) Age 27, single. An American paramedic serving as an ambulanceman in Reno, Nevada. He reached an altitude of 26,000ft on the 1984 Bristol Cho Oyu expedition – his first time to the Himalaya. Jeff has also climbed extensively in Alaska and the American Rockies, and is a competition skier.

Harry McAulay (Travel Officer) Age 33, married. A building services consultant who served a short service commission with the Royal Marines. An all-round sportsman, achieving a high standard at anything he puts his hand to, Harry has in the past taken a particular interest in aikido, judo, boxing and rugby. He started climbing with the Royal Marines eight years ago, and was the Base Camp manager on the Cho Oyu expedition.

Steven Monks (Equipment Officer) Age 26, single. The most experienced climber in the team and a qualified British Mountain Guide. In 1985 Steve made the second British solo ascent of the North Face of the Eiger. He is the author of the current Avon Gorge guidebook and has a wealth of new rock climbs to his credit. He has spent long periods living and climbing in Australia, where his ascents of the hardest climbs earnt him the reputation of being the best climber in the continent. He was the only member of the team to have been on two previous Himalayan expeditions with Steve Berry.

Yeshey Wangchuck (Bhutanese climber) Age 30, married. The best mountaineer in Bhutan, having made a number of first ascents with visiting Japanese expeditions. Yeshey received training in Japan in climbing techniques. He works as an Assistant Manager in the Mountaineering and Trekking Section of the Bhutanese Tourism Corporation, and accompanied the team as a climber and liaison officer. In 1985 he took part in the first attempt on Gangkar Punsum with the Japanese expedition, reaching a height of 22,000ft on the south ridge.

163

Support Trekkers

Maggie Mosey Payne (Trekking Organiser) Canadian. Qualified nurse and inveterate world traveller. Her husband worked as a project manager for a Saudi Arabian sheik.

Tan MacKay (Press Officer) Chief Press Officer for the *Reader's Digest*, she made an enormous contribution to raising funds and producing publicity for the expedition.

John Knowles Age 44, single. Runs his own office supplies business near Oxford.

Peter Santamera Age 42, single. Merchant navy marine engineer living in the Lake District.

Brian Lee Age 40, married. Owns a garden centre near Leicester. Previously had made a guided ascent of the Matterhorn.

Dave Carbis Age 34, single. Runs his own computer consultancy firm; lives near Hemel Hempstead. A keen marathon runner.

Jeremy Knight-Adams Age 39, single. Director in a family-owned property development company; lives in the Cotswolds.

Harry Jensen Age 40, single. An American technician for a body scanner in a hospital in Saudi Arabia. Extremely keen on photography.

Karl Taylor Age 37, single. An American emergency-room doctor from Reno, Nevada. Jeff Jackson's landlord!

Sunday Times Reporter

Peter Godwin Early thirties, single. Now running the *Sunday Times* office in South Africa.

The Film Crew

Alan Jewhurst (Director) Co-owner of Chameleon Film Services, Leeds, who were contracted by John Gau Productions, London, to make a documentary of the expedition for Channel 4 and *National Geographic*'s American cable network, Explorer.

Chris Lister (Soundman) Co-owner of Chameleon. Among many films on adventurous subjects Chris and Alan have produced films concerning Everest, K2, Trango Tower, and Chris Bonington's life story.

Peter MacPherson (Cameraman) Main cameraman for a number of climbing and subaqua diving films.

Mark Stokes (Assistant) Youngest expedition member at 19. Assisted mainly with sound recording.

Ole Fink Larsen (Researcher/Interviewer) A Dutchman living in America who runs 'self-actualisation' courses. Ole was brought in to research our characters, I think.

Bibliography

Ashley Eden, B.H. *Political Missions to Bootan* (Manjusre, Delhi)

Aris, M. *The Early History of a Himalayan Kingdom* (Roli Books International, Delhi, 1979)

Aris, M. *Views oa Medieval Bhutan* (Roli Books International, Delhi)

Chapman, F.S. *Memoirs of a Mountaineer* (Chatto & Windus, 1945)

Colister, Peter *Bhutan and the British* (Serindia Publications, London)

Das, Nirmala *The Dragon Country* (Orient Longman, New Delhi, 1973)

Fletcher, H.R. *A Quest for Flowers* (Edinburgh, 1975)

Hickman, Kate *Dreams of the Peaceful Dragon* (Victor Gollancz, London, 1987)

Mehra, G.N. *Bhutan, Land of the Peaceful Dragon* (Vikas Publishing House, Delhi, 1974)

Olschak, B., Gansser, U., and Gansser, A. *Bhutan* (London and New York, 1971)

Olschak, B. *Ancient Bhutan* (Swiss Foundation for Alpine Research, Zurich)

Peissel, M. *Lords and Lamas* (London, 1970)

Ronaldshay, The Earl of *Lands of the Thunderbolt: Sikkim, Chumbi and Bhutan* (London, 1923)

Rose, L.E. *The Politics of Bhutan* (Ithaca, USA, 1977)

Bhutan: The Dragon Kingdom in Crises (Oxford University Press, Delhi, 1978)

Steele, P. *Two and Two Halves to Bhutan* (London, 1970)

Turner, Captain S. *An Accountant of an Embassy to the Court of the Teshoo Lama in Tibet* (London, 1806)

Van Strydonck, Guy *Bhutan – A Kingdom in the Eastern Himalayas*

Ward, M. *In this Short Span* (London, 1972)

White, J.C. *Sikkim and Bhutan* (London, 1909)